The Nature of Play

A HANDBOOK OF NATURE-BASED ACTIVITIES FOR ALL SEASONS

A Fanny & Alexander book

Created by: Delfina Aguilar
Writer/Editor: Clare Aitken
Designer: Charlotte Coulais/En Ville Studio
Mood illustrator: Sabrina Arnault
Technical illustrator: Hiromi Suzuki
Recipe writer: Katja Tausig
Sub-editor: Louise Banbury

Typeface: Antwerp, designed by A2-Type
& GT Haptik, designed by Grilli Type

Paper supplied by GF Smith
Printed by Push, London, UK
Second printed edition 2020
ISBN: 978·1·9161679·0·2

MIX
Paper from
responsible sources
FSC® C011203
FSC
www.fsc.org

fannyandalexander.co.uk
©Fanny & Alexander, London, 2019

For Silas

—

Spring

Summer

Autumn

Winter

INTRODUCTION

I have always loved bookshops, and
for many years, I wandered their shelves
in search of a book I imagined; first
for myself as a child, then for younger
cousins, then nieces and nephews, and
most recently, for my son. Eventually,
I realised I might have to write it.

I have always loved bookshops, and
for many years, I wandered their shelves
in search of a book I imagined; first
for myself as a child, then for younger
cousins, then nieces and nephews, and
most recently, for my son. Eventually,
I realised I might have to write it.

This is a book of ideas for play that
will offer you excitement, discovery,
creativity and happy immersion through
the year. From summer celebrations
outdoors to quiet rainy day pastimes, it's
full of simple, flexible suggestions for
enjoying more time together and more
of the nature around us (even – perhaps
especially! – in cities). Few activities
require anything other than some time,

curiosity and materials you already have
at home, and most can be attempted
within minutes of landing on the page.
Some activities will be familiar – many
have been tested by several generations
and have withstood the test of time when
much else has changed. It's a book that
will grow with you – each time you flip
through its pages, I hope it will spark
fresh enthusiasm.

Many children don't know how to
play without a screen – this book is a
small inoculation against that state of
being. It requires children to challenge
themselves, find solutions and rely
on their skills and imaginations. Most
of all, it asks them to slow their pace

enough to really observe, to examine, to contemplate and to wonder.

I grew up in Buenos Aires, in Argentina. I remember feeling that the adults were always preoccupied with grown-up conversations and pursuits, and the children were left to play. This was a gift in many ways – it gave me plenty of time for my imagination to flourish. I liked to be solitary, and I often played indoors – several Christmases in a row, my parents gave me a bike, but I steadfastly refused to learn to ride it! I preferred the games that let my imagination unfurl: happily painting, drawing and building cardboard models of our neighbourhood for hours at a time.

Some of my favourites are in this book, like elastics (page 208) and Tuttifrutti (which I still play now for fun with friends at dinner!).

But my father also had a farm outside the city where we often spent weekends. From lazy days spent cooking, to helping take care of the animals, its slower pace always came as a welcome relief. Summers promised a different kind of wildness – my family would often decamp to Urguay's unspoiled coastline. The rest of the year round, I longed for summer's daily walk to the market and hours spent roaming freely outdoors.

That sense of autonomy and awareness of nature are, I think, more vital for children now than ever. The pace of life is faster, entertainment more commercialised and passive, and lifestyles more constrained and urban. This book is a tool: a lever to be used to prise open the window in that airless version of childhood, and allow you to escape into the great beyond of nature and imagination (if only for a few minutes…).

It isn't a definitive guide to outdoor activities or a nature almanac, and nor does it offer operating instructions for children! It's a selection of ideas for playing in, with and around nature, through the seasons, in ways that are as easy as they are enriching.

My hope is that you will reach for it, refer to it and keep it with you for many years. But the book itself is not the point: if you forget the book, but remember moments you spent together exploring its activities, its work will have been done.

— Delfina Aguilar Benitez

BEFORE WE BEGIN

Just before we dive into the activities, there are a few things to bear in mind that will make your adventures and activities a little easier, safer and more fun.

THINGS TO GATHER

Having the right equipment ready makes it easy to set off on an adventure. Try to have the following kit tidily stored and you'll be ready at a moment's notice.

. Appropriate clothing for the season (raincoat, rain boots, gloves, hat and scarf for cold weather; sunhat and sunscreen for warmer days)
. A small rucksack or bag for expeditions
. A lunchbox and water bottle
. Magnifying glass
. Compass
. Old sheets or blankets for building dens or picnicking on
. Craft kit (paper, envelopes, fabric, markers, paints, scissors and tape)
. Notebook for thoughts and observations

THINGS TO COLLECT

Keep your eyes open for materials you can use for your creations. Ask your friends and family to save you anything you particularly want or like.

. Leaves and flowers (you can press these between heavy books to dry out, if you like)
. Shells and feathers
. Ribbons, wool, string and fabric scraps and trimmings
. Cardboard boxes of all shapes and sizes (from matchboxes to big appliance boxes)
. Interesting papers
. Old cards, postcards, and pictures snipped from magazines

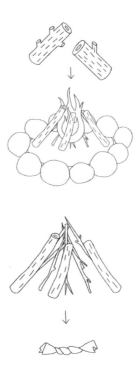

THINGS TO KNOW

Whether you're whiling away a lazy afternoon or pretending you're a castaway on a desert island, a few simple skills will help you conquer all sorts of challenges.

The skills themselves are simple, but once you've mastered them you can use them in all sorts of situations. Can you use your knots to make a life-raft? Can you make an animal menagerie from paper using your origami skills? If you can start a fire, you could try camping out overnight next – the possibilities are endless.

How to start a fire

Starting a fire must only be done once you have a thorough understanding of how to do it safely (and always with an adult's knowledge). Once you've chosen a site that's completely cleared of brush, twigs or leaves, and far from any overhanging foliage, you should create a boundary for the edge of your fire, either by digging a fire pit 30cm deep, or by building it inside a ring of rocks. Next, layer scrunched paper with small twigs in a teepee formation, before carefully lighting the paper at your fire's core. Add other sticks (and eventually logs) in gradually increasing size, making sure the flames have plenty of material to burn, and plenty of air circulation around its core.

The bowline knot

The tautline hitch

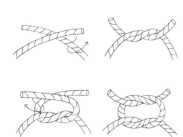

The square knot

How to tie three knots

After you've taken 10 minutes to learn to tie these three knots, you'll wonder how you did without them before! The square knot is also called a 'reef knot' by the sailors who use it to tighten sails in high winds – but you'll be able to use it in all sorts of conditions. This one works especially well if the two threads you want to join are roughly the same thickness.

The bowline knot is a simple way to create a useful loop that won't slip. You can use it to hang something from a hook or tree branch, to haul objects, or even to secure a boat to its moorings.

The tautline hitch is really useful because you can adjust the diameter and tightness of the knot. The most common use for this knot is to tie a tent rope to a peg in the ground – but we're sure you'll find plenty of other uses for it, too.

How to fold basic origami shapes

If you haven't tried it before, you'll be amazed at the origami creations you'll be able to make using simple paper. From detailed animals to beautiful containers, all you need is some paper and plenty of patience.

Almost any paper is suitable for origami, provided it's thick enough to hold a nice sharp crease – but do try to save any unusual or pretty papers you find to make some really special pieces.

How to draw anything

Anything you can draw is made up of three basic shapes: squares, triangles and circles. The trick is learning how to see these shapes in something complicated you're looking at. First, look at the object's main structure and sketch that out. Next, add details you notice, again using the three basic shapes. Once you've sketched the main outline, go back and tidy it up, rounding off corners, erasing any joins between shapes and adding finer details.

THINGS TO REMEMBER

Bear in mind these few simple rules when you're about to start a new activity to make sure you stay safe, preserve your tools and keep everyone happy.

. If you're working on top of a table or piece of furniture, put down newspaper or a mat underneath to avoid any damage.

. Put anything you're going to cut on a firm, flat surface.

. Once you've finished making something, clean up, wash your tools, tightly replace lids on markers or paints and put your supplies away neatly.

. Check the weather forecast before you go out, and dress appropriately.

. Always tell an adult where you're going.

. Leave no trace behind: if you've been outdoors, make sure not to leave any litter or food behind. If you've lit a fire, make sure it's completely extinguished before you leave.

. Don't disturb the animals! If you're outdoors, try not to overturn old logs or boulders as they often provide important homes for bugs. Never approach or disturb nesting birds – they won't be happy, and they'll let you know about it...

. Ask for help if you need to. Each activity is labelled (see below) if you might need adult assistance, so always ask if you need it.

Adult assistance required ••

Spring

EAT

Rhubarb *(rheum rhabarbarum)*

. Is actually a vegetable (except in the US, where, for tax purposes, it's a fruit. Strange, but true)!
. Has poisonous leaves.
. Was brought to Europe from Asia by Marco Polo.
. Has medicinal qualities that made it incredibly precious in the 16th century.
. Can be used to make paper.

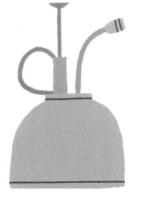

DO

Plant herbs

. Fill the cups of an egg carton with healthy soil.
. Put up to five seeds in each cup.
. Cover with a light layer of soil.
. Spray daily with water to keep moist.
. Place in a sunny spot indoors.
. Plant out when seedlings are 5cm tall.

LOOK
Butterfly watching
It's the perfect time to spot butterflies either waking up from a long hibernation or emerging from their chrysalises. On a warm day (above 20°C), look for flowery places and you'll likely find some of these specimens:

Northern hemisphere:
. Mourning cloak
. Large and small white
. Common blue
. Painted lady

Southern hemisphere:
. Grass yellow
. Monarch
. Bush brown
. Leafwing

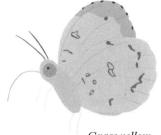

Grass yellow

Large and small white

Bush brown

READ
. *It Starts With a Seed* by Laura Knowles
. *Spring* by Gerda Muller
. *Everything You Need For A Treehouse* by Carter Higgins

TODAY

If ever there were a spring day so perfect,
So uplifted by a warm intermittent breeze

That it made you want to throw
Open all the windows in the house

And unlatch the door to the canary's cage,
Indeed, rip the little door from its jamb,

A day when the cool brick paths
And the garden bursting with peonies

Seemed so etched in sunlight
That you felt like taking

A hammer to the glass paperweight
On the living room end table,

Releasing the inhabitants
From their snow-covered cottage

So they could walk out,
Holding hands and squinting

Into this larger dome of blue and white,
Well, today is just that kind of day.

— Billy Collins

DRINKING SHRUB

A 'shrub' is a delicious, zingy cordial that
you can flavour with seasonal fruits and
add to water for a refreshing drink at any
time of year.

10 MINUTES PREP
7 DAYS FERMENTATION

INGREDIENTS
450g fresh, seasonal fruit
400ml raw apple cider vinegar
100ml freshly squeezed lemon juice
150ml honey or 150g cane sugar
Sparkling water and ice to serve

Sterilise a 1-litre jar by putting it into
the oven at 120°C for 10 minutes (ask
an adult to help).

Put your fruit in the cooled, sterilised
jar and pour your raw apple cider vinegar
over the top.

Cover the jar opening with a small
square of muslin cloth and secure with
a rubber band.

Leave for one day at room temperature.
On day two, put the lid on the jar and
give it a good shake, then leave the lid
slightly ajar.

Leave for six days, shaking (with the lid
firmly screwed on!) every day.

Strain through a fine sieve and discard
the fruit.

Add lemon juice and cane sugar or
honey. Screw lid on well and shake
to dissolve.

Store in the fridge. Add 1 cup of
sparkling water to 2 tbsp of your
shrub to serve. Cheers!

Make seed bombs

Bring blooms to life in the most unlikely corners of your neighbourhood.

GATHER TOGETHER

. Flower seeds (more varieties means
  greater choice of forage for bees.
  Look for local seed mixes that
  are suitable for your environment)
. Peat-free compost or potting mix
. Clay
. Cup of water
. Large bowl
. Baking tray

THE PERFECT TIME TO
SCATTER YOUR SEED BOMBS
IS RIGHT BEFORE IT RAINS.

LET'S GO!

Step 1. Cover a table with a cloth or newspaper and collect all of your materials together.

Step 2. In your bowl, combine about five handfuls of compost with a handful of seeds and mix together.

Step 3. With wet hands, break off about five handfuls of clay, and then tear into smaller, walnut-sized pieces. Place on the baking tray for now.

Step 4. Dribble a small amount of water into your compost mix, until it's just damp (not soaked). Use your hands to roughly mix, then add your pieces of clay and knead, squeeze and squish quickly until it's well combined.

Step 5. Take a handful of the mix and form ping-pong-ball-sized pieces.

Step 6. Place on the baking tray, and leave somewhere warm to dry for at least 3 hours.

Step 7. Take them to the streets! The perfect time to scatter your seed bombs is right before it rains, so that the seeds get plenty of water to help them get started. Think about where they can go: neglected garden beds at your home or school, vacant lots or the bases of neighbourhood trees are all good places to start.

FROM THE ARCHIVES

Seed bombs are often used by 'guerrilla gardeners' to beautify unloved patches of public land. The movement – and seed bombs themselves – began in New York in the 1970s, when the city was in the grip of a financial crisis and public spaces, especially parks, were woefully neglected. Founded by Liz Christy, the Green Guerrillas decided to take matters into their own hands, using their own time and resources to turn abandoned building sites into flourishing meadows of wildflowers and greenery. They'd lob the seed bombs they made over fences into disused lots to give locals something beautiful to look at instead of rubble, an act of urban activism that you're continuing today.

DEAR GROWN-UPS

Although they can be planted in your beds or window boxes, seed bombs were designed as an act of civic generosity and, if you choose to use them this way, are an opportunity to think about community citizenship as well as learning some fundamentals of gardening. Be aware, though, that in some places, acts of cultivation on land you don't own might be regarded as vandalism, regardless of whether they're an improvement on what's already there, so please use your own judgement.

MAKE SEED BOMBS

Get to know a tree

Habitat, weather vane, lookout –
your favourite tree is much busier
than you think...

GATHER TOGETHER
. Magnifying glass
. Pencil
. Notebook
. Leaf chart (overleaf)

LET'S GO!

Step 1. Find a great tree. Take a good look around your garden, neighbourhood or local park to find a tree that looks good for climbing (one with some low branches or good footholds, and some nice boughs for perching in).

Step 2. Stand back from your tree. Is there one side that's bushier or bigger than the other? The bigger side is probably facing south if you're in the northern hemisphere (north if you're in the southern hemisphere). That's because the tree grows more strongly towards the sun.

Step 3. Standing near the trunk, look upwards. Can you see any patterns in the way the branches spread out from the trunk?

Step 4. Carefully climb your tree and find a safe place to rest. If possible, you might like to sit astride a wide branch, and lean back against the trunk.

Step 5. Do you have company? It's not only birds that like to live in trees – can you spot a squirrel's nest, or 'drey'? What about a snail, centipede or caterpillar? Can you identify a stag beetle, or a grasshopper, or a shield bug? If you look closely, you should find that your tree is teeming with busy life. Note down and sketch your discoveries.

Step 6. Using your magnifying glass, look at the leaves to work out what kind of tree you've chosen, using the references over the page. Perhaps you'd like to start a leaf collection in the pages of your notebook.

DID YOU KNOW TREES CAN PREDICT
THE WEATHER? IF SOME OF THE
LEAVES HAVE TURNED UPSIDE
DOWN, THERE MIGHT BE A STORM
ON THE WAY.

Step 7. Did you know trees can predict the weather? If some of the leaves have turned upside down, there might be a storm on the way. (Leaves with soft stems will often become limp and flip over in the humidity change that precedes a storm.) If a pine cone is open, the weather is likely to stay dry, while a closed pine cone means rain is on its way.

Step 8. Map the location of your tree in your notebook so that you can visit it again. Which creatures can you find in the different seasons?

FROM THE ARCHIVES
Trees' branches aren't just lofty perches. They're incredibly intricate plumbing systems that ferry water, sugar and hormones from the roots to the twigs, regulating their growth and signalling when to produce fruit, flowers or leaves. Ancient trees can also tell you about what your local area's climate was like in the past – the concentric rings within the trunk are wider in warm, wet years and thinner in cold or dry years, so scientists can use them to find out whether there were droughts, floods or other wild weather in the days long before humans kept a record.

Beech *Alder* *Ash* *Hazel*

Horse chestnut *Oak* *Field maple* *Hawthorn*

—

DEAR GROWN-UPS

Almost every adult can recall the magic of exploring a tree – the sense of freedom, seclusion and adventure. Playgrounds don't get much more analogue, or adventurous, than this. As well as the chance to climb, balance and swing from the branches, they also reveal incredible secrets and complex communities to the patient observer (and an opportunity for fast-paced children to slow down to a literal snail's pace, too...).

—
Up to 3 hours
All seasons
Indoors
Adult assistance required ••

Create a scene

Set the stage and who knows
what tales might unfold?

GATHER TOGETHER
. A sturdy cardboard box (ideally
  measuring around 30cm x 30cm x 30cm)
. Sticky tape
. Craft glue
. Scissors
. Coloured paper and cardboard
. Scraps of fabric, old wallpaper
  and wrapping paper
. Washable paints
. Egg cartons, matches and
  wooden lollipop sticks
. Felt–tip pens

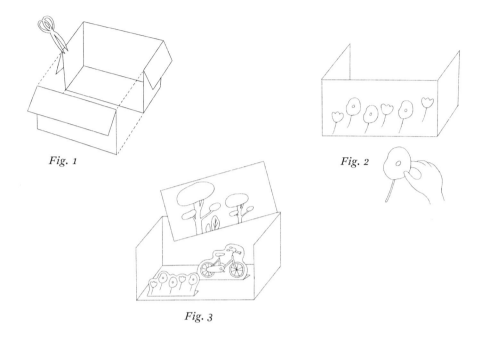

Fig. 1

Fig. 2

Fig. 3

LET'S GO!

Step 1. Choose your scene. You're going to make a set, like a theatre backdrop, for staging plays of your own creation. So the first thing you need to do is to think about what kind of scene you're inspired by. A forest bathed in moonlight, perhaps? An underwater scene in Atlantis? A Victorian doll's house? Or how about the surface of a never-before-seen planet?

Step 2. Get your box ready. Trim off any flaps you don't need (see Fig. 1), reinforce any joins with tape, and decorate the outside of your box in keeping with your theme (see Fig. 2). Note that most marker pen colours will look dark and drab on cardboard, so for brighter colours, glue on coloured paper.

Step 3. Decorate the backdrop. Line the box with wallpaper or patterned paper, or paint it. You can glue on other materials for texture, too – maybe moss and twigs for a forest scene, blue cellophane and shells for your underwater backdrop, or tinfoil for a cosmic landscape. Let your imagination run wild!

Step 4. Decorate the 'stage'. You can do this two ways:

Diorama-style, where you create staggered rows to create a sense of depth. For instance, if you're creating a forest, use a piece of stiff paper to draw and cut out lots of trees and boulders, leaving a small 'foot' (about an inch) at the bottom of each one. Fold the 'foot' and glue it to the bottom of your scene towards the back, positioning it so that

it stands up by itself. Repeat until you have a back row, then glue in a new row of trees a few inches further forward (see Fig.3). It creates a lovely 3D effect.
Dollhouse-style: This is where you use your space as a room and furnish it how you like. Making the furniture is the fun part – matchsticks can be glued together to build bed frames, chairs and tables and matchboxes can be stacked to form drawers. Egg cartons can be cut to build sofas and armchairs, and lollipop sticks can be used to make fridges, wardrobes – or anything you like! Sew or glue pieces of fabric to create pillows, blankets and rugs.

FROM THE ARCHIVES
Although they're beloved by many children, dollhouses were actually invented for adults. The earliest dollhouses were called 'cabinet houses' and were created as status symbols for wealthy Dutch, German and English aristocracy. Later on, the 'baby house' was created for children. They were perfect, scaled-down replicas of the family homes they lived in, and they were used to teach daughters how to run their future households. Luckily for you, yours is purely for fun!

DOLLHOUSES WEREN'T ALWAYS
THE THEATRES FOR CHILDREN'S
IMAGINATIONS THAT THEY ARE
TODAY...

—

DEAR GROWN-UPS

As you have read, dollhouses weren't always the theatres for children's imaginations that they are today. But that's what makes them such enduringly magical things – they're kingdoms over which children have complete dominion. They can explore alternative realities, inhabit others' points of view, replay real scenarios with different outcomes – using their imaginations to develop the social skills that help them to navigate the real world.

—
All seasons
Indoors and outdoors
Adult assistance required ••

Tune up your bicycle

Keep your bike primed and ready
for adventures.

GATHER TOGETHER
. A bicycle pump (if you don't have one,
  your local bicycle shop may let you
  use theirs)
. Allen keys
. Cleaning cloths — sponges and rags
. An old toothbrush
. Dishwashing liquid
. A big bowl of warm water
. Chain oil

LET'S GO!

Step 1. Make sure you're wearing old clothes and, if you're working inside, have laid an old drop cloth, tarpaulin or newspaper on the floor beneath your bike.

Step 2. Check your tyres' pressure by giving them a firm squeeze. If they yield beneath your fingers, they need a top-up. The correct pressure should be printed somewhere on the tyre walls. Pump them to this level and close the valve caps tightly.

Step 3. Check your saddle – does it swivel or wobble? If you've grown a lot lately, it might be time to raise it, too. Use an allen key to loosen it enough to increase the saddle height, and tighten it again afterwards.

Step 4. Give your brakes a squeeze. They shouldn't be too stiff but they shouldn't be too soft either – if you can squeeze them all the way to the handles they need adjusting. An adult (or friendly bike shop owner) can help you do this. Remember to adjust both front and rear brakes evenly so you don't tumble over the handlebars!

Step 5. Clean your bike chain. Flip your bike upside down to balance on the saddle. Use the old toothbrush to loosen any mud or dirt that's stuck on to the chain, and carefully wipe the length of the chain with an old cloth.

Step 6. Give your bike a good wash. Add a few drops of dishwashing liquid to the bowl of warm soapy water and

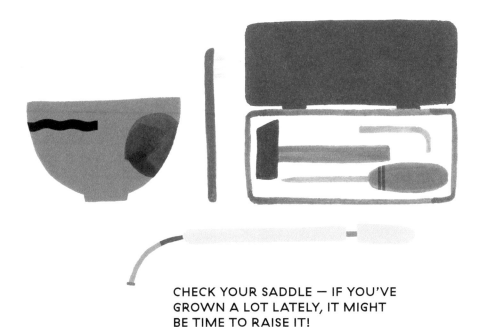

CHECK YOUR SADDLE — IF YOU'VE GROWN A LOT LATELY, IT MIGHT BE TIME TO RAISE IT!

use your sponge to clean off any dirt and mud from the frame and wheels – use your toothbrush again to get around the spokes, brake pads and gears.

Step 7. Flip your bike back over again so that it's the right way up. Bounce it gently to shake the water off. Use a dry cloth to wipe the seat and frame.

Step 8. Leaning your bike carefully against a wall, turn your pedals slowly backwards while you hold the nozzle of your chain oil against the chain's teeth. As the chain turns, you'll reach the entire length. Wipe off any excess oil with a clean, dry cloth – too much oil on the chain will collect dirt.

Step 9. Give your lights a fresh change of batteries.

Step 10. Take your pristine new bike for a spin! It's the best way to dry off any moisture – and it's the best way to enjoy your smooth new ride.

FROM THE ARCHIVES

The Tour de France – a 3,500km cycling race around France – is one of the world's biggest sporting spectacles, with nearly one third of the world's population tuning in to watch. Although today's competitors are honed to physical perfection, early riders habitually smoked as they rode, and stopped in local taverns to guzzle beer. Today's rider will typically lose an incredible 130 litres of sweat during the race, and use up nearly 124,000 calories.

DEAR GROWN-UPS

The benefits of bicycling are almost self-evident: fewer emissions, less road congestion and better-exercised riders. But cycling's greatest gift is perhaps the sense of freedom and independence it offers children, developing physical skills of balance, fitness and endurance but also fostering self-reliance and enabling discovery.

Make a paper plane

Let your imagination take wing!

GATHER TOGETHER
. A4 paper
. Sticky tape

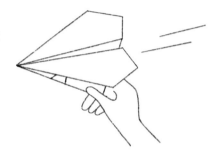

LET'S GO!

Step 1. Fold a single sheet of A4 paper in half widthways, then open it out again. (See diagram on following page.)

Step 2. Fold the top two corners down to meet the central crease you've just made.

Step 3. Fold the peak of your triangle down to meet the previous fold.

Step 4. Take the right and left hand edges of your paper and fold them in so that they touch the central line.

Step 5. Flip your plane over, and fold about 1/2 inch/ 1.5cm of the top edge down to make a 'nose'.

Step 6. Fold the plane in half lengthways.

Step 7. Fold each 'wing' back evenly, leaving a central 'spine' about 2 inches wide – you'll need to grip the plane here to launch it.

Step 8. If you'd like to strengthen your plane, use small strips of tape to seal the centre of the plane between the wings.

Step 9. Lift-off! Try bending the tail up or down to control its direction, or bend one wing up and the other down to make it fly in a spiral.

PAPER PLANES HAVE BEEN USED
THROUGHOUT HISTORY TO
PROTOTYPE FLYING MACHINES.

FROM THE ARCHIVES

Paper planes aren't just great for testing out your folding skills; they've also been used throughout history to prototype flying machines that have eventually taken to the skies. Leonardo da Vinci made models of his 'flying machines' from parchment, and aviation pioneers including Clément Ader and Alberto Santos-Dumont used paper to test out their initial ideas for some of the aircraft that went on to revolutionise flight.

DEAR GROWN-UPS

Making paper planes is a great way to practise the fine motor skills required for folding, as well as the gross motor skills required to fly them. But it's also a chance to practise resilience and analytical skills, working out how to alter velocity or direction, or how to increase flight distance. Even better than these indisputable benefits, though, is that knowing how to fold and fly a paper plane is an instant antidote to boredom that requires only a sheet of paper.

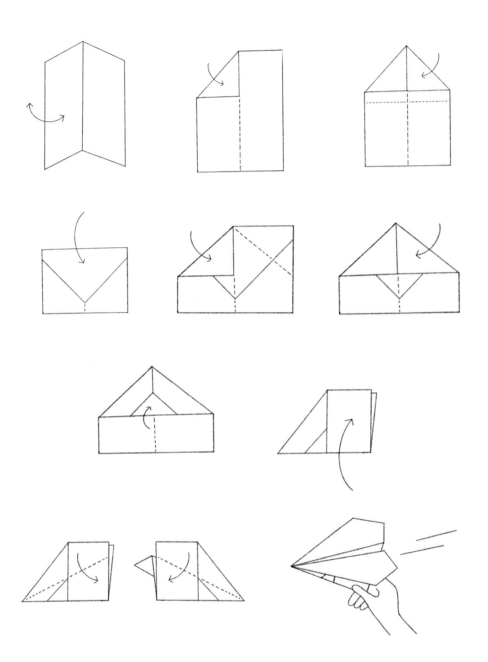

JOHN COLLINS
AKA the Paper Airplane Guy

OCCUPATION
Paper airplane engineer

CAREER HIGHLIGHTS
Setting a new Guinness Book
World Record!

ADVICE
There's no substitute for touching,
manipulating and imagining

What's so special to you about paper airplanes?
Paper airplanes invite play and experimentation. One of the things I do is to float a perfectly made paper airplane over a crowd of people. Almost invariably, the person who catches the plane begins adjusting it. I love that! The world record-holder just launched a plane towards you and, because it's just a paper airplane, you automatically think you can make it better. In what other field of endeavour would people so casually disregard world-class expertise? It's a laboratory to try out ideas and design experiments.

What does a paper airplane engineer actually do all day?
I'll do about 90 to 100 presentations each year. For each one, I'll inspect and test fly the planes at home, remake any problem planes, test fly in the performance space, and then I get to do the show. I also do a fair number of corporate gigs and keynote speeches.

What's the highest and furthest you've ever flown a paper airplane?
I've actually thrown beyond the previous world record [of 69.14 metres, which John co-holds with his 'thrower', former arena football quarterback Joe Ayoob] about three times. I've thrown a paper airplane in an aircraft travelling at

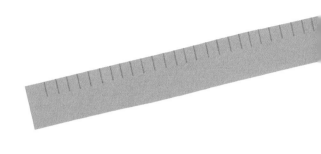

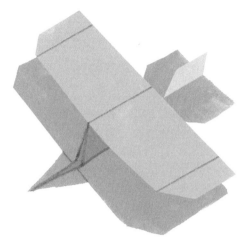

around 9,150 metres in the sky. Does that count as the highest? From ground level, I've had airplanes catch thermals and fly more than 100 feet high.

How does a paper airplane actually work? Do paper airplanes work in the same way as the real kind?
There's still a robust debate about how wings work, so, when someone asks, "How does a paper airplane actually work?" I have to be somewhat vague about the lift question. The NASA website has switched from a Bernoulli explanation to a redirected airflow explanation. Al Bowers, chief scientist at the Neil A. Armstrong Flight Research Center, claims the Bernoulli

explanation is closer to the truth. So, with NASA in disagreement with itself, I'm at a loss to give a definitive answer!

Who invented the paper airplane, and how have they changed since?
People are fond of believing that Leonardo Da Vinci invented the paper airplane because of one tiny sketch in one of his notebooks. It's possible. But it's also possible that paper airplanes came from China, where paper was invented around 250 AD.

The World Record Paper Airplane and International Award Winning Designs, is available now at good bookstores.

Rig up a slingshot

Take aim with your own simple slingshot –
for target practice only!

GATHER TOGETHER
. A forked branch
. Sandpaper
. Rubber bands (the larger and thicker
  the better)
. A scrap of leather or sturdy cloth
. Empty tin cans or a large sheet
  of paper and some marker pens

LET'S GO!

Step 1. Find your branch. Look for a sturdy branch with an open V-shaped fork and a nice straight, smooth handle to grip.

Step 2. Prepare your frame. Break off (or ask an adult to cut off) any twigs growing from the main branch part, and snap (or have an adult cut) the handle down to about 20cm long. Strip any loose bark, and use a piece of sandpaper to smooth out lumps and bumps.

Step 3. Make your band by creating a chain. Lay two rubber bands down so they overlap in the middle. Loop the bottom rubber band through itself and pull tight (Fig. 2). Continue adding other rubber bands to your chain until it's about 25cm long.

Step 4. Make your pocket. Cut a small oval (about 2 inches long) out of your scrap leather or fabric, and poke a small hole on each side at the widest point.

Step 5. Assemble your slingshot. Thread the rubber string through both holes of your pocket. Tie each end to the fork.

Step 6. Take aim! *Slingshots can be dangerous*. Never, ever take a shot indoors, or at any living thing – you could cause serious damage or injury. The best way to practise is to line up a series of cans several metres away, or draw a target on paper and hang it from a fence. Put your ammunition (nuts or grapes are ideal, and they feed wildlife afterwards) in the pocket, draw back the pocket and band, and release to fire.

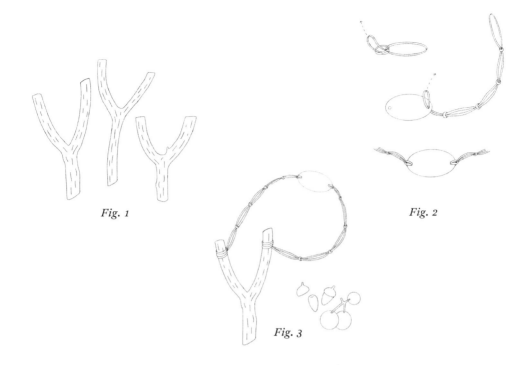

Fig. 1

Fig. 2

Fig. 3

FROM THE ARCHIVES

Slingshots (also called shanghais or catapults in the UK, or gings in the Antipodes) let you shoot an object further than you could throw it, thanks to the extra force applied by the rubber band. As soon as it's fired, your missile's course is affected by gravity, which starts to curve your missile's path down towards the earth. Air resistance stunts its journey, too: if there was no air resistance, it would travel twice as far.

DEAR GROWN-UPS

You might question the wisdom in advocating that children learn how to make their own weapons – but actually, that's the point. Children like to test their limitations, and to attempt dangerous feats. It's how they realise new skills and physical prowess. Even more importantly, trusting children with something inherently dangerous fosters vital self-discipline, which in turn breeds pride, trustworthiness and a sense of independence. Sometimes there's great value in letting (well-supervised!) children toe the line between safety and danger.

—
30 minutes
All seasons
Indoors
Adult assistance required ••

Craft a pop-up card

Add another dimension to your card-making skills.

GATHER TOGETHER
. Two pieces of A4 coloured card
  or thick paper
. Scissors — either children's scissors
  or ask an adult to help
. Glue stick
. Coloured paper
. Decorations (washi tape, glitter, sequins,
  dried flowers — whatever you like)
. Marker pens

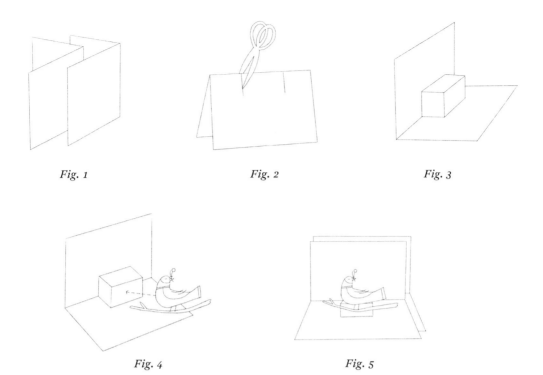

Fig. 1

Fig. 2

Fig. 3

Fig. 4

Fig. 5

LET'S GO!

Step 1. Prepare your cards. Choose a sheet of card for the outside and another for the inside, and fold them both in half so they slot inside one another (Fig. 1).

Step 2. Create your pop-up support. Take the card you want to go inside and, keeping it folded, make two inch-long cuts through the fold, about an inch apart (Fig. 2). Open the card and, from behind, push the tab you've just cut towards you so that it pops out (Fig. 3). Run your fingers along the crease to strengthen the fold.

Step 3. Make your pop-up image. What will pop out from your card? A special message? A picture? Draw or write it on a fresh piece of card and cut it out (it should be no bigger than 8cm x 10cm so

that it hides out of sight inside.)

Step 4. Assemble your pop-up. With your card open, apply some glue to the bottom of the folded pop-up tab and stick on your cut-out so that the bottom is level with the bottom of the tab (Fig. 4). Press well to stick it down.

Step 5. Glue your cards together. Rub glue across the back of your inner card, avoiding the tab. Take your outer card and carefully line up the two cards, then press down well to stick (Fig. 5). Give it 10 minutes to dry.

Step 6. Decorate your card. Use your favourite materials to make the outside of your card look as special as the inside. And don't forget to personalise it with your message!

THE MAGIC OF A SPECIAL PIECE
OF POST DESERVES PRESERVING.

FROM THE ARCHIVES

Pop-up books are generally aimed at children now, but they were originally invented as a way of communicating complex or three-dimensional concepts to adults. In the 14th century, medical students used them as a way of learning all about the human body in detail, and designers such as the landscape architect Capability Brown used them as a way of modelling plans.

DEAR GROWN-UPS

Writing letters and cards is something of a dying art in our digital times for adults and children alike. But the magic of a special piece of post, particularly a handmade one, deserves preserving. Thank you cards and letters are an opportunity to practise appreciation and thankfulness, but newsy correspondence or a no-reason-at-all card is just as lovely to give or receive.

—
Up to 3 hours
Spring and summer
Indoors and outdoors

Plan a picnic

A good meal eaten outdoors is
its own reason to celebrate.

GATHER TOGETHER
. A blanket or throw
. Picnic basket or bag
. Plates, cups and utensils (use enamel
  or plastic versions from home, but
  don't bring your family china!)
. Napkins
. An ice pack or frozen bottle of water
. Two bags for rubbish
. Food and drinks (see notes below)
. Games (cards, board games like Twister
  or bat-and-ball might be fun)

LET'S GO!
Step 1. Choose your destination.
There's something magical about eating
outdoors whether it's on a mountainside
or a park bench. Think about your
favourite patches of nature near you.
Is there a river, hillside or woodland?
Or perhaps an urban park or a friend's
back garden? Look out for posters or
advertisements in your local press:
an outdoor festival or cinema screening
makes an ideal excuse for picnicking.
Step 2. Decide on your menu. Now that
you've got a place in mind, think about
what you'd like to eat. If it's going to
be hot, refreshing salads, simple tarts
and cold drinks might work. If it's cool,
warm pastries and hot chocolate might
be more appetising. Try to think of

foods that are tasty served around room
temperature, and fairly robust dishes
that won't collapse or crumble when you
transport them.
Step 3. Pack it up. Use lidded containers
that won't leak. Glass jars are great
for storing salad dressings (wait until
you get to your picnic spot to add your
dressing or your salad will be soggy), and
plastic or stainless steel lunchboxes and
baking trays are useful, too. Keep drinks
and food cool by packing alongside an
ice pack or bottle of frozen water. Rinse
and cut any fruit at home and pack in
containers. See how little waste you can
produce, avoiding plastic wrap and bags
– try brown paper bags, wrap things
in parchment and tie with string, or tie

THERE'S SOMETHING MAGICAL ABOUT EATING OUTDOORS WHETHER IT'S ON A MOUNTAINSIDE OR A PARK BENCH.

whole fruit or bread into clean tea towels (see our 'wrapping' activity on page 183 to see how).

Step 4. Settle in. Bring a picnic blanket or throw for everyone to sit on. Arrange your food in the centre, with serving utensils and plates on hand. Dress and toss any salads, serve up drinks (the drinking shrub on page 21 is delicious with chilled sparkling water!) and unpack any games you've brought.

Step 5. Tidy up. After you've tucked in, soaked up the great outdoors and worn yourselves out, it's time to pack up and head home. Scrape plates as clean as you can and wrap them in a plastic carrier bag to wash at home – you can also put any recyclables in here, like empty bottles or cans. Use your second bag to collect any non-recyclable rubbish and drop it in a nearby bin. Look back as you leave – you should have left no trace.

GRILLED VEGETABLES WITH WHIPPED RICOTTA DIP

20 MINS PREP
50—60 MINS COOKING

INGREDIENTS
. Small radishes and beetroot cut into
  1cm wedges
. Baby carrots
. Cauliflower, broken into large pieces
. Fresh thyme
. Olive oil
. Salt and pepper

RICOTTA DIPS
. 15g pine nuts
. 15g parmesan cheese, grated
. 25g fresh basil
. 50ml olive oil
. 1 clove of garlic
. 250g ricotta
. 1 tsp lemon zest
. 1 tsp lemon juice
. Salt and pepper

Ask an adult to preheat your oven to
200°C. Place your vegetables in a mixing
bowl, add 3 tablespoons of olive oil, salt
and pepper and a few pinches of fresh
thyme leaves and mix well. Place on
a baking tray and roast in the oven for
20 minutes. Turn all your vegetables
over, and return to the oven for another
20-30 minutes. While they cook, make
your ricotta dip.

Put the first five of the dip ingredients
in a food processor and whiz together.
Scrape the contents into a mixing bowl
and add all remaining ingredients.
Mix well with a spoon and serve
alongside your roasted vegetables.

SUMMER ROLLS

30 MINS
PREP
20 MINS
ASSEMBLY

INGREDIENTS
. Rice paper wrappers
. Rice vermicelli noodles
. Vegetables (an avocado, 2 carrots,
  and ¼ cucumber)
  cut into thin strips
. 2 tbsp roasted peanuts, chopped
. 2 sprigs mint, chopped
. Handful coriander, chopped

Boil the noodles in salted water for about 5 minutes, drain well and allow to cool. Submerge a rice paper wrapper in a bowl of fairly hot water for about 15 seconds until it becomes soft, then lay on a cutting board. In the centre of the wrapper, arrange a tidy mound of the sliced vegetables, vermicelli noodles, peanuts and herbs. Fold the bottom of the wrap over the filling to enclose it, then fold the sides inwards, and roll the wrap so that it resembles a spring roll. Serve with sweet chilli dipping sauce.

FROM THE ARCHIVES

Picnicking supposedly has its origins as a lunch on-the-go for the upper class during their hunts but it was the French who really embraced it (and even named it, coining the term 'pique-nique') when their parks were reopened to the public in 1789 following the revolution. Brilliant picnic traditions abound around the world. On May Day, the Finns tuck into herring and schnapps, while Brits might bite into a Scotch egg. Many cultures picnic in cemeteries so that their loved ones can be part of the fun even after death. And the games vary, too: Greek families fly kites after their traditional picnics on the first day of Lent, while Scandinavians embark on epic games of *kubb*.

DEAR GROWN-UPS

Children are often guests at picnics, but inviting them to organise their own lets them exercise both creative and practical thinking. It's an opportunity to play host, to be considerate of other people's preferences, to act autonomously and to set the agenda. If you're lucky enough to be invited, it's a wonderful way to while away a few hours together, slowing down to enjoy the languorous pace of an afternoon with nowhere else to be.

—
1 minute to 1 hour
All year
Indoors and outdoors

River races

Simple craft for water-powered fun

GATHER TOGETHER
. Two thick sticks for the raft base
. A handful of smaller sticks
. Small piece of paper or fabric
  for a sail
. String
. Hot glue (if you have it)
. Scissors

LET'S GO!

Step 1. Consider your raft design. How big would you like to make it? Will its size make it go faster or slower, do you think? Would you like it to have a mast or a sail? What do you want it to do: travel quickly, carry some cargo, or to outlast the other craft?

Step 2. Build your raft base. Start by cutting or snapping your two thicker sticks to the same length. Lie them down parallel to each other, as far apart as you'd like your raft to be wide.

Step 3. Create the deck. Cut or snap twigs to about 2cm longer than the distance between your base sticks (you want a centimetre of overhang at each end). Take your first twig and place it on top of the base twig (Fig. 1).

Cut a long piece of string – about 1 metre long. Tie one end firmly onto the end of your base stick and then wrap it several times in an 'x' shape around the end of the deck twig (Fig. 2). Keeping the string taut, place the second twig alongside, and repeat the 'x' binding. Continue until your raft is as wide as you want it to be, then tie the string tightly and trim any excess. Cut another length of string and repeat to bind the other side of the deck to the base (Fig. 3).

Step 4. Add a mast and sail (if you'd like). Cut or snap a twig to the size you want (plus an extra 2cm to tuck it into the deck). Cut your sailcloth into your chosen shape and then fix it to your mast – you could fold over and glue one edge

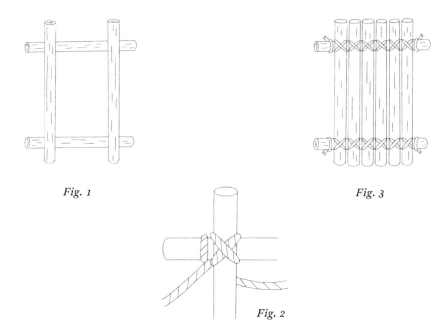

Fig. 1

Fig. 3

Fig. 2

to create a pocket for your mast to slide into (Fig. 4), tie it to the mast or poke holes in it and thread it on. Push your mast between the deck twigs and tie it securely in place (Fig. 5).
Step 5. Set sail. Find a stream or body of water near you (a river, lake or swimming pool will work, but getting your boat back might be tricky!). There are no right or wrong conditions, but think about how the wind or rain or current might affect its course. Lower it into the water and let go. You're away!

N.B. If you don't have time to make a proper raft, try the traditional British game of 'Poohsticks' (named after beloved children's character Winnie the Pooh) instead. Players choose differently shaped twigs and all drop them into the water from a bridge at the same time. The current picks all the twigs up and the owner of the first twig to pass an agreed 'finish line' is the winner.

Fig. 4

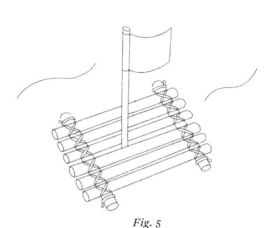

Fig. 5

THINK ABOUT HOW THE WIND
OR RAIN OR CURRENT MIGHT
AFFECT ITS COURSE.

FROM THE ARCHIVES

Manmade rafts like these have provided transport for humans for many centuries, but natural rafts have been doing the same for animal life for aeons. The scientific name for this is 'oceanic dispersal', and it occurs when creatures (or in some cases, plants) cling to natural rafts made from clumps of plant matter that drift out to sea. It's how thousands of species have colonised land masses separated by oceans, eventually arriving on dry land and adapting to the local conditions. After the tsunami in 2011, more than 280 Japanese marine species hitched a ride thousands of miles across the Pacific Ocean, eventually washing up in Oregon, USA — so never underestimate the power of a good raft.

DEAR GROWN-UPS

There's a reason why we're so drawn to the coasts, rivers or lakes of the world — the sight and sound of water induce a cognitive calm that's more important than ever in our frenetic lives. But besides creating the impetus for spending time stream-side, this activity presents challenges of problem solving and dexterity, as well as firsthand exploration of concepts such as flotation and hydrodynamics.

RIVER RACES

Dye your own Easter eggs

Natural dyes make a display of pretty pastel eggs.

LET'S GO!

Step 1. Choose your colours.

Please note: many of these recipes need boiling water or use of a stove – please ask an adult for help if you aren't usually allowed to do this yourself.

Blue. Put 1/4 red cabbage cut into chunks into a pan filled with four cups of boiling water. Add two tablespoons of white vinegar and turn off the heat. Cool to room temperature and remove the cabbage from the pan. Soak the eggs in the water overnight.

Grey–blue. Add a cup of frozen blueberries to a cup of warm water. When the mixture comes to room temperature, remove the blueberries (when they're drained, they're perfect for pancakes or snacks!) and soak your eggs in the coloured water overnight.

Lavender. Mix a cup of grape juice with a tablespoon of white vinegar and soak your eggs overnight.

Pale pink. Take one cup of juice from canned beetroot and add one tablespoon of white vinegar. Soak eggs overnight (or less time for a gentler hue).

Golden brown. Simmer two tablespoons of dill seeds in a cup of water for 15 minutes. Strain the liquid through a sieve into a small bowl, and add two teaspoons of white vinegar. Add your eggs to the liquid and leave overnight.

Mustard yellow. Add two tablespoons of turmeric powder and two teaspoons of white vinegar to a cup of boiling water and stir. Add your eggs.

GATHER TOGETHER

. As many eggs as you'd like to dye
. Several tubs or bowls (one for each dye)
. The ingredients for your colours of
  choice (see below)

Green. Put the skins of six red onions into a pan with two cups of water and simmer on the stove for 15 minutes. Remove the skins and add three teaspoons of white vinegar to the pan. Soak your eggs overnight in the liquid.
Step 2. Store your eggs. Once they've reached your desired colour (leaving them for longer will result in a deeper dye, while less time will mean they're paler), take them out of the dye, pat them dry gently with a paper towel, and store in the fridge until you want to put them on display.
Step 3. Eat them! Don't forget to use your eggs after you've displayed them – unless they're cracked, they shouldn't have absorbed any of the flavours of the dyes, so you can still use the raw eggs in any recipe you like – scrambled or poached, custard or cake, the options are almost endless!

EGG-DYEING HAS BEEN AROUND
FOR CENTURIES. IT'S STILL A
GENTLE, MAGIC TRICK TO SEE
THEM TRANSFORMED.

FROM THE ARCHIVES

Eggs don't give much away, so if you want to know if yours are fresh, just pop them in a bowl of room temperature water. If it lies on its side at the bottom of the bowl, it's fresh. If it stands on one end at the bottom, it's okay to eat, but do it quickly (or hard-boil it). If it floats to the top, it's old and shouldn't be eaten. That's because eggshells are porous (full of lots of minuscule holes) so the older they get, the more air enters the shell, which makes them float. If only it was as easy to solve the age-old question: which came first, the chicken or the egg?

DEAR GROWN-UPS

Egg-dyeing has been around for centuries – it's still a gentle, magic trick to see them transformed using only scraps of vegetables, water and time. You probably have most of the materials on hand, so you can try it out on any rainy day, though it's especially sweet at Easter. Try your own experiments, too – use wax crayons to create pictures on your egg's surface or whatever spices you have in your cup-board. The end product may be pretty, but it's the playing that's the point.

Summer

EAT

Strawberries *(fragaria x ananassa)*
. Are a member of the rose family.
. Are not technically berries – they're
  a thickened part of the stem.
. Are covered in 'seeds' that aren't
  actually seeds! Botanists consider each
'seed' to be a fruit itself, and it contains
its own seeds inside.
. Have superpowers, boosting eye
  and brain function, and reducing
  blood pressure, arthritis, gout and
  cardiovascular disease.
. Do not continue to ripen after picking,
  unlike most other fruit.

DO

Collect and save seeds
. Collect your seeds on a dry day.
. Wait until the seedhead (the plant's pod,
  capsule or nut) is ripe.
. Pick them and dry them somewhere
  warm indoors.
. Collect the seeds: crush tougher
  seedheads gently, or shake flowerheads
  into a paper bag.
. Clean off any chaff and store in a labelled
  envelope somewhere cool and dry.
. Plant next Spring!

LOOK

Cloud-watching

Clouds often get a bad rap for 'spoiling' a summer's day, but summer offers up some magical examples of clouds. Look out for:

. Cirrus: wispy, streak-like clouds at the highest point of the troposphere
. Cirrostratus: very high, thin clouds that look almost foggy, and can create 'sun dogs'.
. Cirrocumulus: little puffy 'cotton wool ball' clouds – these tend to mean a change in weather conditions, so rain might not be far behind.
. Cumulus: the classic fluffy cloud shape you probably draw most often!
. Noctilucent: these remarkable 'night-shining' clouds are only visible during twilight when the sinking sun illuminates them from below the horizon.

Cirrocumulus

Cirrostratus

Cumulus

Cirrus

READ

. *Over and Under the Pond* by Kate Messner
. *A Perfect Day* by Lane Smith
. *Come On, Rain!* by Karen Hesse

SUMMER STARS

Bend low again, night of summer stars.

So near you are, sky of summer stars,

So near, a long-arm man can pick off stars,

Pick off what he wants in the sky bowl,

So near you are, summer stars,

So near, strumming, strumming,

So lazy and hum-strumming.

— Carl Sandburg

ICE LOLLIES

Save your pocket money and still have delicious ice lollies to eat all summer long: it's a win–win situation!

20 MINS
PREP
8 HOURS
FREEZING

INGREDIENTS
100g chia seeds
100ml coconut milk
250g of ripe summer fruit
(berries, peaches, mangoes
or nectarines are all lovely)
500g unsweetened coconut yoghurt
(or your other favourite kind)
60g honey

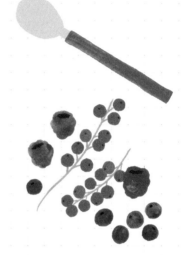

Put the chia seeds into a bowl with the coconut milk and leave for 10 minutes. Meanwhile, put your ripe summer fruit into a food processor or blender and whiz quickly to break it down but not puree it.

Add your blended fruit to the chia seed mix, and add the coconut yoghurt and honey.

Mix well and pour into lolly moulds, adding a pop stick to each one.

Freeze for 8 hours. Run warm water over the outside of each mould to release your ice lolly.

Skimming stones

A seemingly magic trick to master.

GATHER TOGETHER
. Stones for skimming
(see instructions)

LET'S GO!

Step 1. Find a relatively calm body of water to practise on. A pond, pool, lake or river is ideal.

Step 2. Carefully choose your stones. You're looking for smooth, flattish stones, roughly the size of the palm of your hand. Round stones tend to be unstable, but triangular or oval rocks work well.

Step 3. Pinch your stone between thumb and middle finger, and hook your index finger along the stone's edge.

Step 4. Take your position facing the water but turned slightly away at an angle.

Step 5. Throw your stone away from you towards the water's surface, keeping your throwing arm and hand as low as possible as you let go. Snap your wrist quickly as you release it to make it spin – the faster your stone is spinning as it hits the water, the better it will skip.

Step 6. Perfect your angle. Skimming stones is all about getting the stone to hit the water at the right angle so that it bounces across the surface, instead of breaking the surface and sinking straight away. The 'magic angle' is 20 degrees, so imagine that you're trying to throw the stone almost parallel to the water's surface, rather than into it.

FROM THE ARCHIVES

Stone skimming exists across cultures and throughout aeons – it's probably one of the oldest games on earth. In England, it's sometimes called 'ducks and drakes', while in Ireland it's called 'stone skiffing'. The Bengali name for the game is 'frog jumps', and in Bulgarian, Greek, Bosnian, Croatian, Serbian, Montenegrin, Spanish, Ukrainian and Telugu it's called 'frogs', too. Finns and Swedes talk about 'throwing a sandwich' while Japanese people refer to it as 'cutting water'. Wherever in the world you're skipping, skimming, skiffing or smutting (Danish) stones, you can be sure that hundreds of other children are also trying to beat the current world record of 88 bounces.

DEAR GROWN-UPS

For only a very minor investment of time and no equipment whatsoever, this game offers up huge gifts to anyone attempting it. As well as enjoying the simple pleasures of being outside, children improve their motor skills and balance, and develop tenacity and self-confidence. But it's also a masterclass in physics principles such as mass, force and speed – one that can be learned on the banks of a river or watching the wind ruffle the surface of a pond. It's also a game that offers the chance for lifelong improvement. Don't be surprised if your children's skills quickly surpass yours!

Make petal paper

Preserve the loveliness of fresh
flowers with pretty pages made
from scrap materials.

GATHER TOGETHER
. A deckle (the mesh frame you use to
  form your sheets of paper. You can buy
  these online, from a craft shop, or make
  your own)
. One cup of non—shiny paper scraps
  (you can use pages from books or newspaper, brown paper bags, tissue paper —
  or whatever you have)
. Two cups of water
. A handful of petals from wilting flowers
. A blender (ideally an old one not used
  for making food anymore)
. A tub or container (big enough for
  your deckle to lie flat in)
. A sponge
. A wallpaper roller (a small rolling pin
  or even a tin can could work, too)
. A wooden board

LET'S GO!

Step 1. Make your paper pulp. Put your cup of paper scraps together with the water in your blender and pulse to start mixing, increasing the speed as you go until you've got a thick puree. Add your petals and blend them into the mixture.

Step 2. Get your tub ready by filling it about a third full with water. Make sure it's deep enough to cover your deckle by an inch. Add your paper slurry and give it a good stir to mix.

Step 3. Submerge your deckle in the mix, moving it in a gentle circular motion to 'catch' the paper mix. Once it looks like it's an even thickness right across the frame, lift the deckle out of the water and let the water drain off.

Step 4. Remove the deckle frame so you're just holding the slurry-covered mesh. Use your sponge to gently press the non-slurry side of the mesh to draw away as much water as possible. Leave to air dry for 15 minutes.

Step 5. Press your paper out of the frame onto your drying board. To do this, push the slurry side of the frame steady against the board and use your roller on the non-slurry side to ease it out. Once you're confident that it's attached to the board properly, gently ease the frame off from one corner, using your fingers to press back down any parts that lift.

Step 6. Use your mesh frame to make more sheets of paper one by one, following steps 3, 4 and 5.

IT'S PAPER THAT ENABLED HUMAN
BEINGS TO WRITE, PRESERVING
AND SHARING KNOWLEDGE.

Step 7. After it's dried a bit but is still damp, use your roller to gently roll out any bubbles or uneven parts of your paper sheets.

Step 8. When it's dry (you can tell because it won't feel cold on your fingertips), peel each sheet very gently off your drying board.

FROM THE ARCHIVES

It's a testament to how important paper is that it's all around us, every day. In fact, it's paper that enabled writing to become human beings' principal way of preserving and sharing knowledge, resulting in the huge cultural and technological advancements of the past two thousand years. But it's the commonplace nature of paper that means we should do our best to use it wisely – for every tonne of paper we recycle, about 17 trees are saved.

THE CONSEQUENCE OF DEVELOPING
A RELATIONSHIP WITH NATURE
IS WANTING TO TAKE CARE OF IT.

—

DEAR GROWN-UPS

Introducing young children to recycling
is an excellent way to ensure that care for
our planet and its resources is ingrained.
As well as using your local recycling
programmes, activities such as this one
can help to prompt other conversations
and positive actions like composting
food waste, or trying to eliminate plastic
usage. The consequence of developing
a relationship with nature is wanting
to take care of it, so an afternoon of
making paper might actually be far
more meaningful than it first seems.

—
1 hour
Spring and summer
Outdoors
•• Adult assistance required

Cook over fire

The simplest – and possibly best –
way to enjoy a summer night feast.

GATHER TOGETHER
. Well-dried twigs, sticks and small logs
  (green wood will get smoky)
. Newspaper
. Matches
. Shovel
. Bucket (and enough water to fill it)
. Metal grill tray (an old one from
  a barbecue or oven, if you have one)
. Cast iron skillet or pot
. Cooking utensils
. Plates and cutlery
. Oven mitts
. Ingredients (see recipe ideas below)

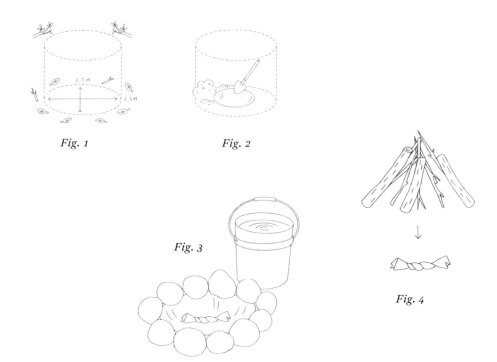

Fig. 1

Fig. 2

Fig. 3

Fig. 4

LET'S GO!

Step 1. Be safe. It's easy for fires to get out of control or become dangerous very quickly, so it's <u>essential</u> that you think and prepare as carefully as possible before you begin. Check for any local fire danger warnings. Don't light fires on hot or windy days (a fairly cool, still day after recent rain is preferable). Make sure an adult is present for this activity.

Step 2. Choose your location. Your backyard is ideal, or a spot on a beach or forest clearing would be lovely too. Find a spot that's sheltered from the wind, where the ground is clear of undergrowth and 2.5 metres clear of any bushes or overhanging branches (Fig. 1).

Step 3. Prepare the ground. Clear away any loose leaves and debris, and use

your shovel to dig a shallow pit (Fig. 2). Use stones to create a ring around the outside of your firepit – this will help to contain the flames. Fill your bucket with water and keep nearby. You'll use this to extinguish your fire.

Step 4. Prepare the fire. Tightly twist sheets of newsprint to make kindling snakes (twisted newspaper will take longer to burn than the scrunched kind) and lay in the centre of your pit (Fig. 3). Lean twigs and small sticks against each other to build a teepee around the kindling (Fig. 4).

Step 5. Ask an adult to carefully light your fire. Fan or blow at the base of the twig teepee to help the fire take, if you need to. As the twigs begin to burn

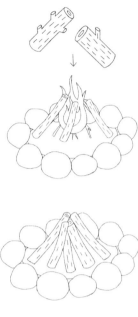

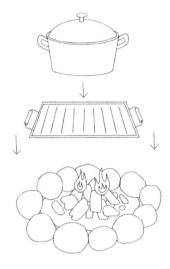

Fig. 5

Fig. 6

down, lean small logs on top to create a bigger teepee shape (Fig. 5).

Step 6. Feed your fire. Keep adding small logs until the fire has plenty of glowing embers at its centre. The heat you need to cook comes from embers, not flames.

Step 7. Get cooking. Once your fire is hot enough, carefully place a grill tray on a stable part of the fire and set your skillet down on top. Always use oven mitts to handle the pot now – it will get very hot very quickly. Cook your favourite campfire classics – see our recipes below for ideas.

Step 8. Put out your fire. Allow your fire to die down gradually and then pour water from your bucket to completely quench it.

PANCAKES

10 MINS PREP
20 MINS COOKING
(MAKES 8)

INGREDIENTS
. 150g plain flour
. 40g sugar
. 1 heaped tsp baking powder
. 2 pinches of salt
. 1 tbsp olive oil
. 1 egg
. 200ml milk

MILK

Mix the flour, sugar, salt and baking powder together in a mixing bowl. In a separate bowl, beat together the egg, milk and olive oil. Pour the wet mixture into the flour, whisking to mix. Let the batter sit for 5 minutes (or longer – you can prepare your mix at home and take it to your campfire in a jar, ready to pour, if you like). Use a little olive oil to prevent sticking, then pour half a ladle's worth of mixture into the pan. Tilt your pan slightly to create the size and thickness of pancake you want. When bubbles start to form (after about a minute), use a spatula to carefully flip it over. Cook for one more minute and serve with fresh fruit and yoghurt, or sprinkle with lemon and sugar.

BARBECUED CORN WITH FLAVOURED BUTTER

10 MINS PREP
40 MINS COOKING

INGREDIENTS
. Fresh corn on the cob (one per person), with outer husk still on
. 90g salted butter at room temperature
. Your preferred flavour combination:

SMOKY HERB BUTTER
. 10g finely chopped herbs (chives/parsley/coriander)
. Grated zest of ½ lemon
. ½ tsp smoked paprika

AROMATIC LIME & GINGER BUTTER
. ½ tbsp lemongrass, finely chopped (white part only)
. 10g coriander, finely chopped
. ½ tsp grated ginger
. Grated zest of ½ lime

HONEY MUSTARD BUTTER
. 1 clove of garlic, minced or finely grated
. 2 tsp honey
. 2 tsp Dijon mustard
. 10g parsley, finely chopped

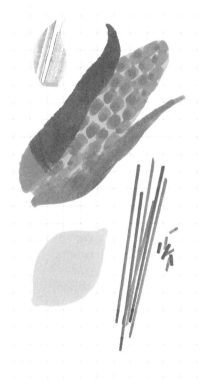

Submerge whole ears of corn in water for 30 minutes before cooking.

Put your soft, room temperature butter in a bowl and add your preferred flavour choices. Mix well until combined, and return to the fridge until it sets firm. After 30 minutes, take it out of the fridge to bring it back to room temperature, and remove corn from water. Place corn on the grill over your hot embers. Cook for 10 minutes on each side, turning carefully with tongs. Use tongs to remove from the fire when cooked, and carefully strip away the husk and any silks. Using either a pastry brush or a small bunch of herbs tied together, brush your cooked corn generously with your flavoured butter. Eat hot!

MIDSUMMER IS A MAGICAL
MOMENT — WHEN A PEBBLE CAST
INTO A BONFIRE CAN MAKE WISHES
COME TRUE.

FROM THE ARCHIVES

If starting and cooking over your own
fire makes you feel clever, you're onto
something – it's thought that the
discovery of cooking over fire between
200,000 and 400,000 years ago gave
prehistoric humans the extra nutrition
and energy they needed to grow bigger
brains. What's more, they even did it
over the exact same kind of fire you're
building today – but your menu is
probably a little more palatable by
today's standards (no woolly mammoth
burgers for you!).

DEAR GROWN-UPS

'Playing with fire' is synonymous with
danger, but when children are taught
to respectfully and carefully make and
use it, they are cultivating remarkably
important skills. It requires patience,
planning and self-preservation and, in
exchange, offers children an incredible
experience of self-sufficiency and self-
confidence. It's also a chance to feel
a sense of custodianship of the natural
world, as children take responsibility
for personal and environmental safety.

Create a time capsule

Stash away a moment in time to rediscover later on.

GATHER TOGETHER
. Container (something sturdy and non–degradable like stainless steel, glass or plastic with a well–fitting lid is ideal)
. Paper
. Pens
. Artefacts (see note below)

LET'S GO!
Step 1. Gather a dozen or so objects that are meaningful to you today (but that you won't need again soon!). Small toys, collectible cards, medals or ribbons you've won, a tooth you've lost or a coin bearing this year's date are all good places to start. Paper tends to break down easily, so if you'd like to include a letter to your future self, a drawing or special tickets, slip them inside plastic sleeves and seal them as tightly as possible with tape. You could write a short story, draw the outline of your hand or take a snap of your current bedroom to go in there, too.

Step 2. Choose a container that's big enough to comfortably house the artefacts you've gathered.

Step 3. As you pack each item in the capsule, make a note of it on a piece of paper. This is your time capsule log. Use it to list the items with a short note explaining a little about what each one is and why you've chosen it.

Step 4. Tucking your time capsule log inside, close and seal your capsule as tightly as possible. If you like, you can decorate the outside of your capsule using permanent markers (if it's going to be outdoors) or paper, paint or fabric (if keeping it indoors). Inscribe it outside with the date you plan to open it. The longer you can wait, the more interesting the contents will be to you when you rediscover it.

Step 5. Decide where your time capsule will be hidden. If you (or one of your friends) have a garden, you could bury it there, or if you'd prefer to keep it safely indoors, find an out-of-the-way corner somewhere warm and dry you don't venture very often and hide it there. **Step 6.** Draw yourself a little map to the capsule's location, and make a note of the opening date. Keep this map somewhere very safe until the time comes to retrieve and open your capsule. You may be fascinated to see how much you've changed (or stayed the same!).

FROM THE ARCHIVES

For thousands of years, time capsules have been used as a way of preserving a moment in time to remind our distant future selves of who, and how, we once were. None are more distant than the ones who might eventually open the two time capsules that are currently orbiting in space! Launched in 1977 aboard the Voyager spacecraft, the Voyager Golden Records are two phonograph records containing images, sounds of nature and human activities, music and greetings in 55 languages, designed to give extraterrestrials a glimpse of life on Earth should they ever be found.

YOU MAY BE FASCINATED TO SEE
HOW MUCH YOU'VE CHANGED
(OR STAYED THE SAME!).

—

DEAR GROWN-UPS

You've probably wished more than
once that you could stop time to enjoy
this moment – especially in fleeting
childhoods – for longer. Time capsules
are a simple way to savour the moment,
both in creating your time capsule with
your child and reflecting on what makes
them who they are right now, as well
as in rediscovering it in years to come.

Go crabbing

Catching (and racing!) crabs should
be summer's official sport.

GATHER TOGETHER
. A couple of rashers of streaky bacon
. Fishing line (a reel or a hand line)
. A fishing net
. A small mesh bag (optional, but
  very helpful)
. A bucket

LET'S GO!
Step 1. Prepare your habitat. Crabbing is all about observing your catch, not eating it, so you need to make them comfortable. Fill your bucket halfway with seawater, and maybe a frond of seaweed and a stone or two (Fig. 1). Keep it in a shady spot out of full sun.
Step 2. Get your bait ready. Cut a rasher of bacon in half and put one half in a mesh bag, if you have one. Pull the drawstring tight, and tie the bag to the end of your fishing line or reel. Otherwise, just tie the bacon directly on to the end of your fishing line (ask an adult for help if you need to) (Fig. 2).
Step 3. Position your bait. The best crabbing spots are on a quay, jetty or harbour wall, or somewhere just above a calm, protected spot in the water. With your net at the ready, gently drop your line into the water until you feel the bait touch the bottom.
Step 4. Catch your crabs. After about five minutes, gently lift the line slightly – it should feel heavier. If so, slowly reel in your line until the bait (hopefully with some crabs attached!) emerges from the water, then scoop it up, crabs and all, in your net.
Step 5. Transfer your crabs. Crabs might look tough, but you need to handle them gently. To stop them moving, press down lightly on their shell (see 'From the archives' below). While they're still, pick them up carefully: put your thumb and one finger either side of the crab's

Fig. 1

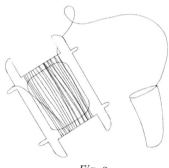

Fig. 2

shell, just behind the base of their pincer legs (Fig. 3). Place them carefully in the bucket. Make sure they're all completely immersed. A wet crab is a happy crab!

Step 6. Get to know your crabs. What can you learn about your crabs? Do they have different markings? Which directions can they move in? Are they male or female? (Turn it upside down to check: males have pointed tails, females' tails are U-shaped.)

Step 7. Set them free again. After a few minutes, you'll need to release them back into the sea (crabs, understandably, don't like to be kept captive for very long). If you want to race them, each person should choose a crab and pick them up carefully as before.

Stand back from the shore and release them at the same time – the first crab to reach the water is the winner (Fig. 4)! Otherwise, just gently tip them out at the water's edge.

83

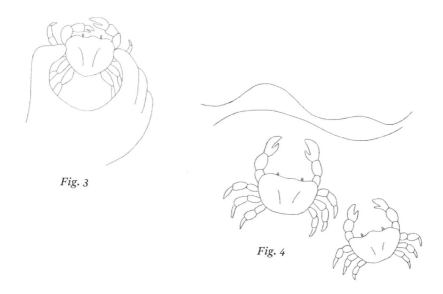

Fig. 3

Fig. 4

FROM THE ARCHIVES

When crabs grow, they outgrow their shells and shed them, legs and all. This process is called 'moulting', and they do it several times over the course of a lifetime. When you pick up a crab, if its shell feels soft, please immediately release it back into the water – a crab's hard shell is its protective suit of armour, so if its new shell hasn't grown in yet it's very vulnerable. Another weapon in the crab's arsenal is, of course, its claws – but did you know that they also use them to communicate? Clever crabs.

DEAR GROWN-UPS

Crabbing is a beautifully fleeting activity, simply a chance to observe at close quarters these intriguing little critters. Practising patience, learning to be gentle and considering the wellbeing of small creatures are the simple, special benefits of this summer pastime.

Weave a simple basket

Make a basket just like people have been doing for aeons.

GATHER TOGETHER

. A roll of brown paper
. A ruler
. A pencil
. Scissors (a child-safe version, or ask an adult to help)
. Sticky tape

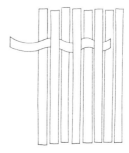

Fig. 1

LET'S GO!

Step 1. Prepare your strips. Using your ruler, mark out and carefully cut (or ask an adult to cut) 16 strips of brown paper each measuring 30cm long and 3cm wide. Cut out another 6 strips measuring 50cm long and 3cm wide. Fold each strip into thirds lengthwise.

Step 2. Form your base. Lie eight of the shorter strips side-by-side horizontally. Lie the other eight shorter strips vertically on top. Take the first vertical strip and weave it alternately over and under the horizontal strips (Fig. 1). Repeat with the other vertical strips, making sure the weave is as close as possible (Fig. 2).

Step 3. Add sides. Fold the strips up along each edge of your base as shown.

Starting from one corner, weave one of your longer strips over and under the loose side strips, creasing at each corner to form a sharp bend (Fig. 3). When you've done a complete row, take another strip and begin a new row above. Keeping adding rows until you have about 1cm of your original base strips still showing above.

Step 4. Tidy it up. Tuck loose ends inside your basket and use a small piece of sticky tape to stick them down as invisibly as you can. Voilà!

THE TECHNIQUES YOU'RE USING
HERE HAVEN'T CHANGED FOR
27,000 YEARS.

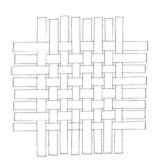

Fig. 2

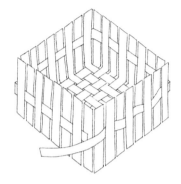

Fig. 3

FROM THE ARCHIVES

Weaving is one of those ancient human skills that transcends place and time – any culture you can think of probably had a tradition of its own. Baskets were invaluable for gathering food, carrying babies, storing things and catching birds or fish, and they could be made using whatever materials could be sourced locally, like reeds, straw, leaves or bark. The techniques you're using here are virtually unchanged from those used to make the earliest known baskets, which date back to 27,000BC.

DEAR GROWN-UPS

As well as producing beautiful, functional objects at the end, the process of weaving is brilliantly meditative, easy to learn and swiftly gratifying. It's such a universal practice, but it can also prompt consideration for the ways in which cultures and humans throughout time are both distinct and different.

WEAVE A SIMPLE BASKET

Games for journeys

Beat backseat boredom as you set off
on your summer holidays.

GATHER TOGETHER
. Blank paper
. Pens or pencils

LET'S GO!
Holidays are surely one of the best things about summertime – but you have to get there first! Having a few brilliant travel games up your sleeve will make the journey fly by.

Tuttifrutti
For as many players as you like
Step 1. Choose 10 categories of things to name, such as countries, animals, something you might buy in a shop, famous people, foods, films, villains, songs, excuses for being late for school – use your imagination!
Step 2. Each person draws a grid on their paper with the 10 categories written down the left hand side, and three columns marked out alongside.

Step 3. Ask someone to silently think through the alphabet until you say stop - the letter they've landed on is the letter you'll use for your first round of answers.
Step 4. When everyone's ready, say 'go!'. Each player must suggest an answer for each category beginning with your chosen letter. Fill in the blanks as quickly as possible. The first person to write an answer for every category shouts 'Stop!' and everyone must immediately put down their pens.
Step 5. Score your answers:
. 0 points if you didn't write anything
. 5 points if you wrote the same answer as another player
. 10 points if you have a unique answer
. 20 points if you're the only player to

have come up with an answer for that category.

Step 6. Choose a letter for your next round and repeat. The highest scorer after three rounds wins.

Battleships

For two players

Step 1. Each player starts by drawing two identical 10x10 grids on their sheet of paper, both labelled 1-10 across the top and A-J down the left-hand side.

Step 2. On the first grid, secretly draw rectangles (either horizontally or vertically, but not diagonally) to represent your fleet of ships:

. 1 x aircraft carrier (5 squares)

. 1 x battleship (4 squares)

. 1 x cruiser (3 squares)

. 2 x destroyers (2 squares each)

. 2 x submarines (1 square each)

Don't let the other player see where you're hiding them!

Step 3. Each player takes it in turns to try to sink the other's ships by calling out a coordinate (for example, C3). If they have a ship in that location, your opponent must say 'hit' and mark it down on their grid. Once you've hit all the squares for a particular ship, your opponent has to tell you which one has been sunk, saying "You've sunk my cruiser" (for example).

Step 4. Use your first grid to mark down any hits on your own ships and the second grid to record your shots at your

IF USING A PENCIL AND PAPER
SEEMS OLD-FASHIONED TO YOU,
YOU'RE RIGHT! PAPER HAS BEEN
AROUND FOR 2,000 YEARS.

opponent, using 'X' to show successful hits and 'O' for misses. The first player to sink all of their opponent's ships wins the game!

Chain Story
For as many players as you like
Step 1. One person starts the story off, beginning with as many exciting twists as possible, stopping right in the middle of a cliffhanger – "and then all of a sudden…" – before tagging the next person to continue.
Step 2. The second storyteller picks up where the first left off, adding their own funny, frightening or dramatic events to the narrative, before passing it along exactly as before.

Step 3. When a storyteller sees an opportunity to cleverly conclude the tale, they should do so. (You might include forfeits for storytellers who use cheap tricks such as 'they all lived happily ever after'!)

Alphabet I-Spy
For as many players as you like
Try to find something corresponding to every letter of the alphabet (in order) as you travel along. All players play in parallel, calling out their 'finds' for each letter, before moving onto the next one. The further into the alphabet you get, the harder it becomes! You might have to think creatively for letters like 'Q' or 'X'… The first to complete A to Z wins!

FROM THE ARCHIVES

If using a pencil and paper seems old-fashioned to you, you'd be right! Paper has been around for nearly 2,000 years, since the Han dynasty started milling it in ancient China. Pencils are positively new-fangled compared with paper, with the modern kind first invented in Germany in 1662. But if you made a mistake and needed to erase your pencil marks before 1839 (when the modern rubber eraser was created) you might have found yourself having to resort to stones, wax, or even bread.

DEAR GROWN-UPS

Although these games should (hopefully!) help to alleviate boredom, being a bit bored every now and then is no bad thing. In fact, occasional boredom has been proven to encourage creativity and nurture the imagination. Long journeys might even be a rare opportunity to have some strange, enlightening or entertaining conversations among the whole family. But if not, there's always another round of 'Alphabet I-Spy'...

Plan a midsummer party

Here comes the sun – let's celebrate!

LET'S GO!

The reason for the season

With the sun shining high in the sky, the flowers in bloom and holidays on the horizon, there's plenty to celebrate in midsummer. In fact, in Scandinavia, it's the biggest celebration of the year after Christmas. A midsummer party is a beautiful way to mark the middle of the year with all the best that the season has to offer.

Decorations

Nature offers up plenty of adornments for making your party special. You could put a few simple wildflowers in jars, or use foliage to create wreaths of greenery, depending on what you have to hand. Ribbons tied to tree branches are another lovely way to set the scene if you'll be outside in a park or garden.

Activities

Flower crowns

You'll need 10 to 20 individual flower stems (about 10cm each) to make a traditional flower crown. Take your first flower and use a fingernail to make a small slit in the stem about an inch from the bottom. Thread the next flower gently through the slit until the flowerhead sits snugly against the first stem. Repeat until you have enough flowers to comfortably wrap around your head, and secure.

GATHER TOGETHER
. Paper and envelopes
  for your invitations
  Flowers and greenery
  for your decorations
. Food and drinks for your
  feast (see recipes below)
. Plates, cutlery, glasses
  and picnic blankets

Boot tossing (also known as 'welly wanging' in the UK!)
Collect several pairs of wellington boots. Stand on a mark and take it in turns to fling a boot as far as you can – experiment with techniques to see which one is most effective. The person who throws the boot furthest is the winner.

Apple bobbing
Fill a large tub with warm water, and float as many apples in it as there are players. Taking it in turns (or all at once if your tub is big enough), players hold their hands behind their backs and try to catch an apple in their mouths, using only their teeth to pick it up. The first player to catch an apple wins.

Sack races
You'll need a large cloth sack or old pillowcase for each person in the race. Each person stands inside their sack on the start line, and when the signal to begin is given, hops their way as fast as they can to the finish line – the first one to cross it is the winner. (If you don't have sacks, try a three-legged race instead: two partners stand side-by-side, arms interlinked, and their inside legs are tied together using a ribbon or scarf. They have to work together to run as fast as they can over the finish line.

Other ideas
Bring games from home. Bocce, Twister, badminton and hula hoops are all fun.

MIDSUMMER IS THOUGHT TO BE
A MAGICAL MOMENT IN THE YEAR —
A TIME WHEN COWS SPEAK AND
ELVES APPEAR.

Feasting

Planning your menu is one of the best parts of hosting a party! In Sweden, they traditionally eat herrings and new potatoes dressed with chives. If pickled fish isn't quite your thing, you could make their midsummer dessert – fresh sponge cake filled with vanilla cream and strawberry jam before being slathered with whipped cream and fresh berries. Celebrate the wonderful food of the season: fresh berries and stone fruits, corn, melon and prawns are all great places to start. Meals that allow everyone to make their own version are perfect: pack plenty of fresh salads, meats and cheeses for a sandwich-making session, or salsas, sour cream, spiced meat and tacos for a fiesta. Don't forget the drinks – elderflower cordial is a summer tradition in the northern hemisphere (see page 21 to make your own cordial), but cold chocolate milk or jugs of iced water with berries and mint could be lovely, too.

Invitations

Now that you've planned your party, all you need are the guests! You could make some petal paper to use for your invitations, or vintage postcards, or decorate your own note-cards and pop in envelopes to send in the mail. Think about what you'd like your guests to know. The date, time and location of your party is essential, but perhaps you'd

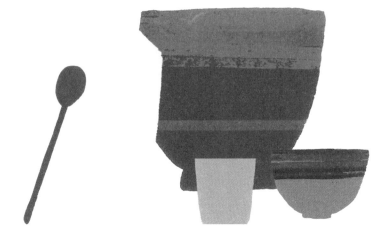

also like your friends to wear or bring something special? Would you like them to let you know if they can make it? (If so, write 'RSVP by [date]'.)

Getting ready
Make sure everything's ready in plenty of time for your guests. If it's outside, spread out some blankets on the grass, or set the table if there is one. Prepare your food ahead of time, and make sure you have glasses, cutlery, plates and serving utensils ready. (Bring these from home and take them home to wash afterwards to avoid creating any waste.) Keep drinks in a cooler or bucket of ice, and, as the Swedes say at their midsummer celebrations, *skål*!

GRILLED FISH AND
FENNEL SALAD

10 MINS
PREP
20 MINS
COOKING

INGREDIENTS

. 1 bulb fennel
. 1 lemon
. Whole white fish (bass or similar)
  cleaned and descaled – for four people,
  use a 1.2kg whole fish or four smaller
  300g fish

DRESSING
. 3 tbsps of extra virgin olive oil
. 1 tbsp white wine vinegar
. 1 tsp mustard
. 1 tsp honey
. 1 tsp capers
. Salt and pepper

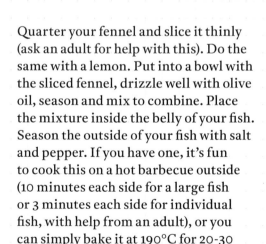

Quarter your fennel and slice it thinly (ask an adult for help with this). Do the same with a lemon. Put into a bowl with the sliced fennel, drizzle well with olive oil, season and mix to combine. Place the mixture inside the belly of your fish. Season the outside of your fish with salt and pepper. If you have one, it's fun to cook this on a hot barbecue outside (10 minutes each side for a large fish or 3 minutes each side for individual fish, with help from an adult), or you can simply bake it at 190°C for 20-30 minutes. To check if it's cooked, push a metal skewer into the thickest part of the fish, pull it out and touch it to your lips. If it's piping hot, the fish is cooked.

While your fish cooks, thinly slice the rest of your fennel and place into a bowl. Put all the dressing ingredients into a jar with a tight-fitting lid, and shake well to mix. Pour over your fennel and stir to coat. Once cooked, place your fish on a big plate, pile your fennel salad on top, and garnish with the soft fronds from the top of your fennel.

BUTTERNUT SQUASH SALAD

**15 MINS
PREP
45 MINS
COOKING**

INGREDIENTS
. 1 small butternut squash
. 1 tsp cinnamon
. Olive oil
. 1 stick celery, thinly sliced
. 2 tbsp sunflower seeds
. 2 tbsp coriander
. 75g soft goats' cheese
  torn into chunks

DRESSING
. 9 tbsp extra virgin olive oil
. 3 tbsp lime
. 2 tsp honey
. Salt and pepper

Preheat the oven to 200°C (ask an adult to help). Cut the butternut squash in half lengthways and then crossways into thick slices. Mix in a bowl with the cinnamon, a big pinch of salt and enough olive oil to coat. Place on a baking tray and roast for 40 minutes, turning halfway through. After 40 minutes, sprinkle over the sunflower seeds and roast for another 5 minutes. While it cooks, combine your dressing ingredients in a small bowl. Leave to cool, then mix with the dressing, celery and half the coriander. Place on a dish and add the goats cheese. Garnish with the remaining coriander.

FROM THE ARCHIVES

Summer solstice, or the longest day
of the year, occurs when either the
northern or southern hemisphere is
tilted as much towards the sun as
it will be all year. For countries closer
to the poles, the sun doesn't even set
on the longest day of the year, making
for magical, surreal nighttime views
(and extra time for staying up late
celebrating). That's probably why
midsummer is thought to be a magical
moment in the year – a time when, in
Iceland, cows are meant to speak and
elves come down from the mountains,
or in Ireland, a pebble cast into a bonfire
can make wishes come true.

DEAR GROWN-UPS

Allowing your child to plan and host
a party is as creative a venture as it is
social. Midsummer is a perfect prompt –
an opportunity to mark the season, enjoy
the light, warmth and freedom of longer
days and explore folklore and traditions
from around the world. Choosing
food encourages children to connect
with where their food comes from and
consider why certain produce is more
readily available, or tastes better, at
particular times of year. It's a seasonal
exploration for all the senses. What's
not to celebrate?

Navigate with nature

Working out where you're headed
can be second nature.

GATHER TOGETHER
. Appropriate clothing to wear
  (hat, waterproof gloves and boots
  in autumn and winter; light layers,
  sunscreen and hat in spring
  and summer)

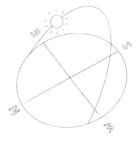

Fig. 1

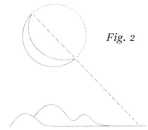

Fig. 2

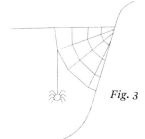

Fig. 3

Fig. 4

LET'S GO!

Natural wayfinding is about learning to read the signs all around us in nature that tell us which way we're facing and where we're going. Master these skills and you'll never be lost again!

The sun

The sun always rises in the east and travels westwards, so if you watch the sun moving across the sky, you can work out east and west. But it's not always 'due east' (which means 'directly east'). Depending on what season it is, the direction will be slightly different because the earth tilts on its axis as it travels around the sun (see Fig. 1). In summer, the sun rises in a more northeasterly position,

and a southeasterly direction in winter, while in spring and autumn the direction is closer to 'due east'.

The crescent moon

When there's a crescent moon high in the sky, draw an imaginary line between the two points of the moon, and then extend it downwards to the horizon (Fig. 2). In the northern hemisphere, that will point you roughly towards the south, or towards the north if you're in the southern hemisphere.

Animals

Animals always prefer a sheltered spot, so look for traces of where animals have stayed – spiders' webs, strands

of sheep's wool, or a sleeping hollow. Find out which direction the wind normally blows from in your area. For instance, if it tends to blow from the southwest (as it does in the UK), these animal traces will usually be on the northeast side of rocks, trees or hillsides (Fig. 3).

Trees

Trees like to grow towards the sun, so if you take a really good look at a tree, you'll notice that it's a bit lopsided (you might have to walk right around it a few times to really spot it). The fuller or denser side will be the part of the tree that gets the most sun (Fig.4) – in the UK, that's the south, so you can work out which is the southerly direction.

FROM THE ARCHIVES

If you have a compass, you'll always know which direction you're facing. But how does it actually work? Well, a compass contains a tiny magnetic pin that swings freely around the dial, responding to Earth's own magnetism. It will always settle and point north because all magnets have both a north and a south pole, and the north pole of one magnet will always be attracted to the south pole of another. So the compass's south pole seeks out and finds the Earth's magnetic north pole, showing us the way. Simple and mindblowing, isn't it?

TREES LIKE TO GROW TOWARDS
THE SUN, SO IF YOU TAKE A REALLY
GOOD LOOK AT A TREE, YOU'LL SEE
IT'S A BIT LOPSIDED.

—

DEAR GROWN-UPS

Many of us live in environments in
which it's hard to get lost because we're
surrounded by signage and mobile
phone maps most of the time. But
learning to use natural signs to navigate
our world is about rediscovering that
we are still living in a wild world with
its own governing principles, restoring
us to a sense of our own intrepidness
in the process.

NAVIGATE WITH NATURE

TRISTAN GOOLEY

OCCUPATION
Natural navigator

CAREER HIGHLIGHTS
Probably the first time I learned to use trees as a map, going back over 20 years now! And, more recently, passing on skills I'd been taught by the Tuareg in the Sahara to Omani guides — sharing indigenous skills from one part of the world with another. [He's too modest to mention it, but he also happens to be the only living person to have both flown and sailed solo across the Atlantic Ocean!]

ADVICE
Don't mistake the map for the world.

How did you become a natural navigator?
I was quite curious as a kid, and I'd think it might be more interesting at the top of the hill than at the bottom, and that the other side of the lake could be more interesting than the side I was on. All that happened was that the hills became mountains and the lakes became oceans! Then I realised that taking big journeys using instruments wasn't nearly as much fun as doing small journeys using nature as my map and compass.

What does a navigator spend the day doing?
These days it's a really fun mix of small journeys and occasional big journeys. Everything I do, whether it's crossing a 100-mile stretch of wilderness or going for a walk in the park or writing a book or putting something on the website, it's learning and discovery and then communicating that. So I could be going for a sail in the morning and giving a talk to a school or a company in the afternoon. I'm very lucky.

When was the last time you got lost?
When I was 19 I walked for three days without food because I got properly lost on the side of a mountain in Indonesia. At least once a week I take myself to an environment I don't know and challenge myself to find my way. I don't see that as being lost but as gathering the information I need to find my way.

Can you use nature to find your way even in a big city?

There are always signs in our surroundings – we just need to broaden our definition of nature. There are usually plant signs, like mosses and lichens and trees, but other signs in the city, like satellite dishes or people, can be useful, too. If you travel against the flow of people in the morning, or with it in the afternoon, you'll find a transport hub. Nothing is random; everything is a sign.

What's the most dangerous situation you've been in?

The most scared I've been is crossing rivers and gullies in Borneo. You're crossing fallen trees that were never meant to be used for walking across, 10 metres above the ground. That's much more frightening than flying a small plane – aviation is all about drills; there's much more opportunity for human error crossing a river!

What's the strangest thing you've ever eaten on an expedition?

The Dayak in Borneo are incredibly pragmatic, and when they hunt, nothing is wasted. It's safe to say I've eaten every edible part of a deer, even the less palatable parts! I also ate a lot of frogs on that trip...

Wild Signs and Star Paths is available now at good bookstores.

INTERVIEW

Hello !

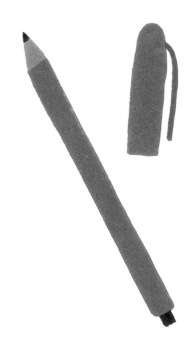

Write a letter

Put pen to paper to master the time-honoured tradition of letter writing.

GATHER TOGETHER
. Stationery — a notecard and envelope or airmail envelopes and sheets of your favourite writing paper
. Stamps (make sure you've got the correct stamps for your destination)
. Pens (experiment to find your favourite)

LET'S GO!

Not so long ago, if you wanted to send a message to somebody, you would have to write them a letter. Although there are lots of ways you can get in touch now, there's a special kind of magic in a handwritten letter.

Step 1. Decide who you're going to write to. Maybe a friend, or relative who lives far away? Perhaps a teacher, or your mum?

Step 2. Decide on the purpose of your letter. You might just want to say hello, or tell them about something that's recently happened to you or a dream you had, or invite them to a party or over to play. Perhaps it's a letter to say thanks for a present, or to ask Santa for a special gift, or to ask your parents to cook you your favourite meal.

Step 3. Start your letter. There are as many different ways to write a letter as there are letter writers! The best kind of letters capture your own unique personality, so you should write them in the way that comes naturally to you. For instance, you can choose how you'd like to begin your letter:

Dear _____ , or *Hi* _____ , or *Hello!*

Step 4. Write your main message. Are you writing as yourself, or is it from an imaginary person? Perhaps you're an astronaut writing a letter from the moon

telling your father all about what you've seen. As you write, think of the person who will be reading your letter – what do you think they will be most interested in hearing about?

Step 5. Sign off. When you come to end your letter, there are even more options. Choose carefully, because it's the last part of your letter so it will stay with your reader. Depending on how well you know them, you could say:

Lots of love, _____ or *Sincerely,* _____ or *Your friend,* _____ or *Kind regards,* _____.

Step 6. Address your envelope. Find out your recipient's full address and carefully write it out on the envelope so the postal workers can read it.

Step 7. Post your letter. Affix the right stamp for your destination (you might need to visit a post office for this part) and drop it in a post box. Off it goes!

IF YOU EVER FIND ONE OF THESE RARE, UPSIDE-DOWN-PLANE STAMPS, SAVE IT — IT'S WORTH ABOUT $1,000,000!

FROM THE ARCHIVES

Before airplanes existed, letters were delivered by other kinds of transport such as trains, boats and ponies. In May 1918, one of the world's first airmail routes began to be operated by the United States Post Office, flying post between Washington D.C., New York and Philadelphia. The stamp for an airmail letter cost 24 cents (a fortune at the time). The stamp was red and blue and had an airplane on it. But by mistake, on some of the stamps that were printed, the airplane was upside down! The upside-down-plane stamps were extremely rare, and people thought they were funny, so they collected them. If you ever accidentally find one, save it — it's worth about $1,000,000!

DEAR GROWN-UPS

Although sitting down to write a letter might seem positively antiquated, the practice encourages imagination and empathy, fine motor skills and penmanship, and the even more important art of pausing to formulate your thoughts and make a personal connection with somebody. Even in our digital age, there are plenty of opportunities to pen a proper letter, and receiving one in the post is even more special because of its rarity.

Construct a sand volcano

Make your own natural wonder – BYO marshmallows!

GATHER TOGETHER
. Twigs
. Scrap newspaper
. Matches
. Marshmallows

LET'S GO!

Step 1. Find your spot on the beach. Choose a spot that's fairly sheltered from the wind and not too close to the water's edge (if the tide's coming in, you'll need to leave an extra margin).

Step 2. Build your volcano. Using your hands to scoop the damp sand, build a large pyramid shape (Fig. 1). You're aiming for a final height that is as long as one of your arms (you'll see why in a moment). Every now and then, give your volcano a good pat all over to make sure it's nice and solid.

Step 3. Create your magma chamber. Once you're happy with the size and shape of your volcano and it's nice and firm all over, slowly start to create a tunnel underneath by pushing your fist

through the sand at the base (Fig. 2). Go steadily, making sure you don't disturb your volcano's foundation too much. Keep tunnelling with your hand as far as you can until it emerges at the other side, or until you can't reach any further (in which case, pull your arm out and, from the opposite side of the volcano, create another tunnel the same way until you meet the first one).

Step 4. Make your pipe. The pipe is the vertical tube in a volcano through which the eruption is funnelled up and outwards. To make yours, stand to one side of your volcano. Find the centre of the top of your volcano, and gently push your fist downwards all the way to the bottom, just like you did with your

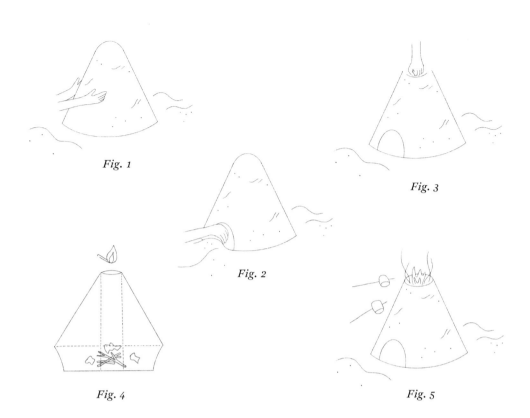

Fig. 1

Fig. 3

Fig. 2

Fig. 4

Fig. 5

magma chamber (Fig. 3). You need to get right to the bottom – that's why your volcano can't be taller than your arm is long!

Step 5. Build your fire. Reach into your magma chamber at the base and clear out any fallen sand. Clear a slightly larger space in the very centre where your magma chamber and pipe meet - but do this very gently so your volcano doesn't collapse! Twist or scrunch pieces of scrap paper and push them into the central hollow. Add some small twigs to the paper pile, and then ask an adult to strike a match and set it alight. As the fire begins to grow, carefully add more twigs to build some heat (Fig. 4).

Step 6. Get toasting. When your volcano is nice and hot, and there's plenty of heat coming up through the pipe, push a marshmallow onto a long stick and hold it above the pipe (Fig. 5) until it's slightly charred outside and gooey inside.

IT'S OFFICIAL — TOASTING
MARSHMALLOWS OVER A LIVE
VOLCANO IS A BAD IDEA.

—

FROM THE ARCHIVES

It's official – toasting marshmallows over a live volcano is a bad idea. A local asked if it was safe to toast marshmallows over a volcano's vent when Hawaii's Kilauea erupted, and the US Geological Survey replied with a resounding no. Not only would it be extremely dangerous, the gases emitted by the volcano would make the marshmallow taste revolting. You might get a pretty special effect, though: according to the USGS, the sulphuric acid would cause a spectacular reaction when it came into contact with sugar.

DEAR GROWN-UPS

Beaches are a wonderland for kids – places where they're often allowed to roam more freely, explore the elements and test rarely used skills. Being allowed to play respectfully with fire engenders trustworthiness and allows children to explore their limits under safe supervision. Being allowed to run a bit wild occasionally is an essential experience, and not only for children.

Autumn

EAT
Pumpkin
. Is a member of the gourd family, which includes watermelon!
. Is technically a fruit, since it contains its seeds.
. Was so named in English for the first time in *Cinderella*.
. Was not the original jack-o-lantern (that was turnips and potatoes).
. Is completely edible – every single part!

DO
Plant bulbs
. Plant before the first frost (before October to be on the safe side).
. Choose healthy, plump bulbs.
. Plant within a week of purchase.
. Choose a spot (in your garden or a pot) with plenty of sunshine and good drainage.
. Place your bulbs about 10cm deep and 5-7cm apart.
. Cover with soil and water well.
. Wait for them to come into springtime bloom!

LOOK

Autumn leaves
Trees' colourful displays in every
shade from flame red to marigold are
one of nature's best annual shows.
Keep a special eye out for:
. Japanese maple
. Hazel
. Rowan
. Wild apple
. Larch
. Acacia

Acacia

Larch

Japanese maple

Rowan

READ

. *Lots* by Nicola Davis
. *Stuck* by Oliver Jeffers
. *The Dangerous Book for Boys* by Conn
  and Hal Iggulden and *The Daring Book
  for Girls* by Andrea J. Buchanan

Hazel

WILLOW POEM

It is a willow when summer is over,

a willow by the river

from which no leaf has fallen nor

bitten by the sun

turned orange or crimson.

The leaves cling and grow paler,

swing and grow paler

over the swirling waters of the river

as if loath to let go,

they are so cool, so drunk with

the swirl of the wind and of the river —

oblivious to winter,

the last to let go and fall

into the water and on the ground.

— William Carlos Williams

FIGS WITH RICOTTA, HONEY, THYME AND ALMONDS

When figs are fresh, they hardly need any preparation — but don't let that stop you trying this amazing combination.

5 MINS
PREP
10 MINS
COOKING

INGREDIENTS
6 ripe figs
6 tbsp fresh ricotta
6 tsp runny honey
2 sprigs of thyme
4 tbsp toasted flaked almonds

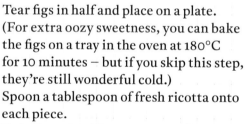

Tear figs in half and place on a plate. (For extra oozy sweetness, you can bake the figs on a tray in the oven at 180°C for 10 minutes – but if you skip this step, they're still wonderful cold.)
Spoon a tablespoon of fresh ricotta onto each piece.
Drizzle each with a teaspoon of honey, and scatter the leaves from two sprigs of thyme, as well as a small handful of toasted flaked almonds, across the plateful. Serve!

Build a den

Whether outdoors or in, every kid needs
(and can make) their own hideaway.

GATHER TOGETHER
. Poles (see below)
. Tarpaulin or old bed sheets
. Rope, string or lengths of elastic
. Snacks (a thermos of hot milk and
  a stash of cookies are our favourite)

LET'S GO!

Step 1. Choose a spot. If the weather's not too windy or wet, there's nothing better than an outdoor den, either in an overgrown corner of your garden, in a local park or nearby woodlands. Indoors, anywhere you'll have a little bit of privacy from the grown-ups is ideal – hideaways are meant to be secret!

Step 2. Decide what kind of structure you'd like to build. All your den needs is a frame and a cover. Try to find a high point to be the starting point for the roof. If you're outside, look for a tree with a good, sturdy trunk. You could build your walls leaning against it, or drape your cover from overhanging branches. Indoors, the high back of a chair or a tabletop will do the trick.

Step 3. Get your structural materials together. Thinking about the structure you've chosen, and gather together poles to build the frame. If you're outdoors, try to find fallen branches of a similar length, or indoors, try broom handles, bamboo canes or the backs of chairs.

Step 4. Build your structure. First, decide where you're going to put your entrance. It should be facing away from the wind (if you're outdoors) to keep it as protected and warm as possible inside. As you begin to form the structure, use your lengths of rope or string to tightly lash the poles together where they meet. And remember: the smaller your den, the cosier and warmer it will be inside.

Step 5. Cover your frame. If you're outdoors, gather more supple, leafy branches and weave them around the structure until it's well covered. If you've got a tarpaulin, drape it over the top and anchor it at the bottom with stones. Indoors, sheets or blankets will create a cosy cover.

Step 6. Make it inviting inside. Line the floor of a forest den with ferns or hay, or even your coats. Make a warm nest in an indoor den with pillows and quilts. Battery operated candles or string lights will make it feel magical. Set out your snacks and enjoy your very own secret den.

Step 7. Leave no trace. When you've finished your den for the day, pack it away. If you're outdoors, take any branches down and scatter them around the site so that woodland critters can use them for shelter once again. Check to make sure there's no evidence of your den lying around. 'Here today, gone tomorrow' is part of the magic!

BUILDING A PLACE TO HIDE AWAY
IS A RARE CHANCE TO CREATE YOUR
OWN KINGDOM.

FROM THE ARCHIVES

Knowing how to build a shelter is an incredibly valuable skill – and one that man has been perfecting for millennia. After living in caves and natural sheltering spots, humans in the Ice Age began experimenting with what they could build themselves, even using mammoth bones for the main supports and its skin for a kind of tent cover. Luckily for the mammoths (who turned out to be quite unlucky in the end, but that's another story), humans moved on to other materials as they began to settle and farm, using sun-dried clay blocks as bricks, or thatched huts made from stone or wattle and daub.

DEAR GROWN-UPS

There's hardly a skill that building a den doesn't provide the opportunity to practise. There are the intellectual and spatial calculations needed for planning; social skills of collaboration, leadership and citizenship to flex; and physical challenges required to build a reliable structure. Once built, it's a place that truly belongs to the child, where they can exercise their independence and let their imaginations run wild. In an age where children are perhaps under more scrutiny than ever before, building a place to hide away is a rare chance to create their own kingdom.

BUILD A DEN

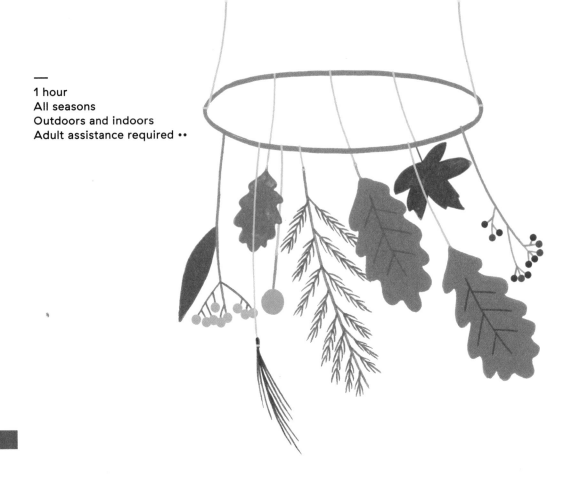

1 hour
All seasons
Outdoors and indoors
Adult assistance required ••

Create a seasonal mobile

Celebrate the turning seasons with
a fluttering natural mobile.

GATHER TOGETHER

. The main structure of your mobile —
  either a long branch or the central frame
  of an embroidery hoop
. Embroidery thread, string or fishing line
. A selection of objects collected from
  nature
. Scissors
. A small nail or screw-in hook
. A small hammer (if you're using a nail)

LET'S GO!

Step 1. Collect your materials. Take a neighbourhood walk and collect what you're going to hang – perhaps rust-coloured leaves in autumn, holly or berries in winter, sprigs of herbs or everlasting flowers – anything you find that catches your eye.

Step 2. One by one, tie a short length of thread to each of your objects and the other end to your mobile structure. Think about where to place them – keep them evenly spaced along your supporting structure, and trim the threads to different lengths that look good together.

Step 3. Hang your mobile. If you're using an embroidery hoop or something circular, you'll need to experiment with different string placements and lengths until it hangs straight – then tie a knot at the top to create the loop your mobile will hang from. Choose a spot on the ceiling where your mobile will catch a gentle breeze if you'd like or a wall if it's a branch you'd like to hang flat. Hold it up to check the placement, then mark the hanging spot with a pencil. Use your hammer (or ask an adult) to gently tap a small picture-hanging nail into the spot you've marked, or screw the hook into your ceiling point. Hang your mobile up by its loop.

Step 4. Change the objects suspended from your mobile as the seasons turn.

MOBILES HAVE A KIND OF MAGIC TO
THEM — WATCHING THEM GENTLY
TURNING IS A MEDITATIVE ACT FOR
CHILDREN AND ADULTS ALIKE.

FROM THE ARCHIVES

Mobiles might seem like child's play, but they're serious art, too. The great artist Man Ray started it all in 1920 with his chandelier made out of 63 coat hangers, followed by Bruno Munari's suspended 'Useless Machines'. Alexander Calder dedicated many years to perfecting mobiles (which he called 'kinetic sculptures') so ingenious that even Albert Einstein was mesmerised. One of Calder's pieces, Poisson Volant [Flying Fish], sold recently for $26,000,000 — so today's work of art could set you on the path to something big.

DEAR GROWN-UPS

Mobiles have a kind of magic to them; watching them gently turning is a meditative act for children and adults alike. Their construction requires fine motor skills, patience, perseverance, and imagination – and, if updated throughout the year, provide an opportunity to connect with the arriving seasons and the passing of time. All this from a branch and some string – a very practical kind of magic, then.

—
30 minutes (with one week for leaf prepa-
ration and 24 hours' drying time)
Autumn
Outdoors and indoors
•• Adult assistance required

Create a leaf mask

Disappear among the trees with your
own leafy disguise.

GATHER TOGETHER

. A selection of leaves — a good mix of colours, shapes and sizes looks great
. Thin cardboard
. Scissors
. Elastic
. Permanent markers (we favour black and white ones with fine tips)
. Glue
. Paintbrush
. Heavy books
. Newspaper

LET'S GO!

Step 1. Get your leaves ready. You can use them as soon as you've collected them, but they'll get crinkly and crumbly very quickly. For a longer lasting mask, lay your leaves out flat on a sheet of paper, lay another sheet of paper on top and sandwich between some heavy books. Leave them for a week to flatten out.

Step 2. Once your leaves are ready, prepare your mask. Draw the shape you want on the cardboard (classic superhero eye mask, or full face?) then carefully cut it out with your scissors (or ask an adult to help). Hold it against your face and mark circles where the eye holes will need to go. Cut them out, too.

Step 3. Fit it to your head. Use a hole punch or a sharp pencil to poke a hole on each side of the mask. Cut a piece of elastic about 30cm long and tie a knot in one end. Thread the loose end through one of the holes and pull it tight. Try the mask on and pull the elastic through the opposite hole so that it fits snugly. Holding the elastic in place, slide the mask off and tie a knot where you've measured it. Trim off any excess.

Step 4. Decorate your mask. First, cut the stems off the leaves. Brush glue onto one leaf at a time, then stick it down onto your mask, taking care not to cover the eyes. Layer your leaves until your mask is completely covered.

Step 5. Leave to dry. Once the glue is completely dry, sandwich your mask between two sheets of newspaper and put a heavy book on top for 24 hours. This will help to make your mask nice and flat.

Step 6. If you like, use your markers to draw on the leaves. Patterns or symbols can make it look extra special. Voilà!

FROM THE ARCHIVES

Trees get all the glory, but leaves are pretty amazing. Did you know that when they change colour in autumn they're actually returning to their normal colours? In summer they're green because all the chlorophyll in their leaves blocks their real, rich rainbow hues. And when they fall off, it's because the tree is essentially cutting them off – leaves contain water that would freeze in the cold weather and damage the fragile inner tree, so the tree creates a seal between itself and its leaves that makes them loosen and fall.

DID YOU KNOW THAT WHEN
LEAVES CHANGE COLOUR IN
AUTUMN, THEY'RE ACTUALLY
RETURNING TO THEIR NORMAL
COLOURS?

—

DEAR GROWN-UPS

Wearing masks and dressing up is an
incredibly rich form of imaginative
play. Pretending to be other characters
is a natural way of developing empathy
for other points of view, and playing
out stories and scenes allows children
to safely explore, and triumph over,
experiences that might make them feel
frightened or helpless. With a dressing
up box, bag or drawer stashed away,
all the world's their stage.

—
1 hour
All seasons
Indoors and outdoors
•• Adult assistance required

Fly a kite

Let your imagination take flight
along with your homemade kite.

GATHER TOGETHER
. Two slender bamboo canes
  (one measuring 60cm,
  one measuring 45cm)
. A large sheet of waxed paper
. Coloured tissue paper
. A handsaw (and an adult to use it!)
. Paper tape
. Ball of string (at least 15m long)
. Some ribbon or scraps of
  coloured paper
. A ruler
. A pencil
. A toothpick
. Glue

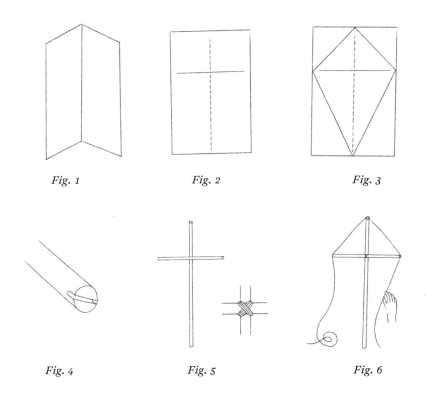

Fig. 1   Fig. 2   Fig. 3

Fig. 4   Fig. 5   Fig. 6

LET'S GO!

Step 1. Make your kite's sail. Cut out a rectangle 60cm long and 45cm wide. Fold the rectangle in half lengthways, then unfold it and lie it flat again (Fig. 1).

Step 2. Use your ruler to measure 15cm from the top along both long sides of your paper, and mark it with a pencil (Fig. 2). Draw a line from the centre points at both the top and bottom to the pencil marks you've just made to end up with a diamond shape (Fig. 3).

Step 3. Carefully cut your diamond out.

Step 4. Ask an adult to cut a small notch in each end of the canes (Fig. 4).

Step 5. Lie the longer cane on the floor, then place the shorter cane across it to form a cross. Tightly wrap string several times around the join and tie (Fig. 5).

Step 6. Take a long piece of string and, starting from the top of the frame, wrap it around the ends of the cross-pole, slotting into the carved notches (Fig. 6). At the bottom, pull the string taut and tie a tight double knot.

Step 7. Lie your paper diamond down, and place the frame on top (Fig. 7). Secure it by glueing down small squares of paper to stick the pole to the sail.

Step 8. Fold the sail's edges down, enclosing the string frame, and seal with pieces of tape (Fig. 8). Leave the knotted end of the string out, and tie on a 2m-long streamer cut from the coloured paper to form a long tail.

Step 9. Use a toothpick to poke a small hole either side of your kite's crossbar

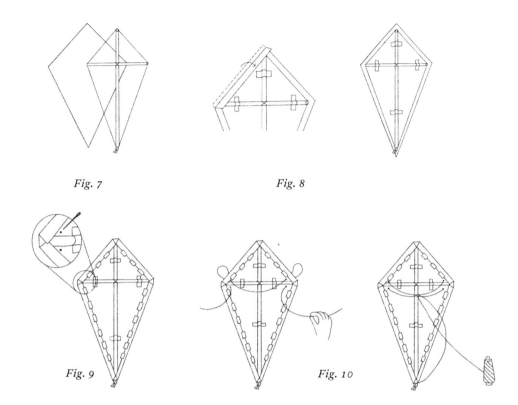

Fig. 7

Fig. 8

Fig. 9

Fig. 10

at each tip (Fig. 9). Thread a small piece of string through each hole and, leaving a small amount of slack in the string, tie securely. Use these loops to thread a 70cm length of string across the kite, tying to the small knots you just made (Fig. 10).

Step 10. Tie the loose end of the remaining ball of string to the centre of this cross-string (Fig. 11). This is the reel you'll use to let your kite soar (and bring it back down to earth again).

Step 11. All that's left to do is decorate the reverse side of your kite. Glue on shapes cut from coloured tissue paper, add leaf prints, or potato stamp it (see page 184) to make it beautiful.

Step 12. Take it outside to an open space away from trees or overhead cables, stand with your back to the wind, and let your kite take wing!

FLY A KITE!

KITES WERE FLOWN BY
BENJAMIN FRANKLIN
TO PROVE THAT LIGHTNING
IS ELECTRICAL.

FROM THE ARCHIVES

Kites existed before paper – the very first ones were made from leaves. Since then, they've been used to hoist materials for building shrines in Japan, and to send military signals in China in the sixth and eighth centuries. Kites have been flown to smuggle goods across borders, to train hunting birds, and even, by Benjamin Franklin, to prove that lightning is electrical.

DEAR GROWN-UPS

There's a reason kites evoke such joy in all of us. Learning to fly them fosters perseverance and pride, as well as giving us the chance to learn about wind and flight. Best of all, we get to enjoy the pure sensations of wind on our cheeks and the happy tug of a kite string in our hands. Making your very own flying machine from scratch feels close to making magic happen. And it's two activities in one: make your kite on a rainy day for indoor fun, then head outdoors when the clouds part to go flying!

Build a bug hotel

Make a welcoming retreat for local creepy
crawlies to weather the winter in.

GATHER TOGETHER

. A wooden box or crate
. Different materials to make various
  'rooms' for the beasties: hollow reeds
  or bamboo for bees (cut to fit the box's
  depth), bark for woodlice and millipedes,
  twigs for beetles and spiders, and
  straw and pinecones for ladybirds and
  lacewings
. Planks of wood or branches
. Bricks

LET'S GO!

Winters are tough for little beasties – by making a bug hotel, you're giving them some-where warm to wait out the worst of the weather and lay their eggs, supporting the insect populations that will be so helpful in your garden come springtime.

Step 1. Create your 'rooms'. Fill one corner of your box with densely packed hollow reeds or bamboo with the holes all pointing outwards – the bees and bugs will crawl into these tubes. Next to that, pack in handfuls of straw, then a section of pinecones, then some twigs, then some leaves. Try to alternate hard and soft materials, solid and porous, packing each section tightly.

Step 2. Add another layer. You can separate the 'floors' of your hotel by cutting planks or sticks to the same width as your box and laying them horizontally. Then, pack the next layer with different sections of materials as before. Remember: it needs to be very tightly filled to keep the minibeasts protected.

Step 3. When your hotel is packed to the top, take it outside and find a suitable spot for it – a quiet area of a park or woodland, or an overgrown garden corner. Stack some bricks evenly beneath each corner to raise it off the ground, and place the box on top with the open side facing forwards.

A DUNG BEETLE CAN PULL AN
OBJECT THAT WEIGHS 1,000 TIMES
MORE THAN HIM — HE'S EARNED
THE RIGHT TO REST.

Step 4. Wait for some guests – once a week through winter, use a magnifying glass to see who's moved in. Be very careful when approaching the box in case any bees have taken up residence. Keep your distance and move calmly and you should be just fine.

FROM THE ARCHIVES
They're not called 'busy bees' for nothing – bees' wings beat more than 11,000 times every single minute, and a single honeybee colony can make up to 100kg of honey each year. Ladybirds also work industriously, eating 5,000 insects over the course of their lifetimes. And one dung beetle can pull an object that weighs 1,000 times more than him – so your guests have more than earned the right to rest their weary bodies at your luxurious bug hotel.

GET TO KNOW THESE AMAZING
CREATURES, FROM PREHISTORIC
DRAGONFLIES TO BUTTERFLIES
THAT TASTE WITH THEIR FEET.

—

DEAR GROWN-UPS

Taking care of the garden's smallest
residents is an opportunity to notice
how hard they work on our behalf,
hoovering up pests, munching debris
and improving the soil. Observing
them through winter is a great regular
incentive to get outdoors, and for
the whole family to get to know more
about these amazing creatures, from
prehistoric dragonflies to butterflies
that taste with their feet – as well as
supporting the ecosystems that help
pollinate the plants when the earth
turns back towards the sun.

Make a flipbook

Drawings come to life with
this simple trick.

GATHER TOGETHER
. A stack of lightweight paper — about 50
  sheets is perfect. You could use a notebook
  or use clips, staples or glue to bind a stack
  of paper yourself
. Drawing materials (pencils, pens and
  any media you'd like to use to add colour)

LET'S GO!
Step 1. Think about what you're going
to draw. A flipbook is the simplest kind
of animation there is – the idea is that
you create a sequence of drawings that
gradually change from page to page so
that when you flip through them quickly
they appear to be moving, just like a
cartoon. (In animations, each picture is
called a 'frame', and up to 60 frames are
played per second.) The first time you try
this, you might like to choose something
simple, like a stick figure jumping up
and down or a sun rising.
Step 2. Create your first drawing. Use
the last page of your notebook – this
will form the starting scene of your
animation, which you'll flip from back
to front. Try to avoid the top left of your
page if you can – when you flip the pages
later, you won't see that area as clearly.
Draw it first in pencil, and then ink over
the top when you're happy with it.
Step 3. Draw your next frame. On the
second-to-last page of your notebook, redraw the same scene as before, but with
one very slight movement. If it's a sun
rising, the whole image should be almost
identical but show the sun slightly higher
in the sky. If it's a stick person, they
might be starting to bend at the knees
a little as they prepare to jump.
Step 4. Continue adding frames.
Page by page, subtle changes should
work towards the overall movement
you're after. Once you've done a few
frames, try flipping through your book

to see how it's coming along to give you an idea of whether you need to make your changes bigger or smaller.

Step 5. Colour it. When the sequence is complete, use paints, pencils or markers to add colour to each frame. As before, the colours should stay the same page-by-page for consistency, but clever changes (the sky behind the rising sun becoming streaked with colour, or your jumping person's cheeks reddening) can make it seem even more lifelike.

Step 6. Flip it! Your animation should play out fairly seamlessly. Now try another one, increasing in complexity now that you've mastered the basics...

FROM THE ARCHIVES

When you watch an animation, it's literally your eyes playing tricks on you, turning a series of still images into a continuous moving image. Filmmakers call this 'persistence of vision'. The human eye and brain can only process 10 to 12 separate images in a second, with each image staying in the brain for a 15th of a second. If another image enters the brain during that time, it overlaps with the previous image and is read as continuous motion. So next time you're watching a movie, consider how many still images you're actually looking at to really boggle your mind's eye.

THE HUMAN EYE AND BRAIN CAN
ONLY PROCESS 10 TO 12 SEPARATE
IMAGES IN A SECOND, WITH EACH
IMAGE STAYING IN THE BRAIN FOR
A 15TH OF A SECOND.

—

DEAR GROWN-UPS

Creating a flipbook conjures a special
kind of wonder: seeing your images come
to life is an eye-widening experience. It's
also a great way to cultivate patience and
problem-solving, requiring the animator
to break down a complex sequence into
a series of smaller gestures and illustrate
them carefully. And, of course, it comes
with all the benefits of any drawing,
from mastering hand/eye coordination
to considering perspective, texture,
depth of field and more.

Take leaf rubbings

Take a leaf out of nature's book with these beautiful imprints.

GATHER TOGETHER
. Paper (any kind and colour will
  do, as long as it's not too thick)
. Wax crayons or pastels
. Soft lead pencils
. A selection of fresh leaves

THE ARTEFACTS YOU'RE CREATING
TODAY COULD BE PORED OVER
BY FUTURE GENERATIONS TO
UNDERSTAND WHAT LIFE RIGHT
NOW WAS LIKE.

LET'S GO!

Step 1. Collect your leaves. Look for beautiful specimens of all shapes and sizes, from dinner plate-sized oak leaves to delicate ferns.

Step 2. Arrange your leaves on a tabletop. Lie them as flat as possible in an arrangement that looks nice to you.

Step 3. Take your print. Lie your paper carefully on top and press down. Using the long edge of a crayon or pastel (not the tip), rub firmly back and forth over the leaf shapes to reveal their pattern and capture all their veiny loveliness.

Step 4. Create different patterns. Use different materials to achieve different effects: a soft lead pencil, with the tip on an angle, will give your print a softly metallic appearance, or you could use different coloured crayons for an autumnal rainbow.

Step 5. What else can you take prints of? Brass plaques and coins work well, but see what else you can find on your expeditions. Can you identify all the leaves you've collected? Your rubbings would make an excellent addition to a nature journal documenting your finds through the year.

FROM THE ARCHIVES

Far from being simple child's play, the origins of crayons go back 3,000 years, when Egyptian and Greek battleships were decorated with coloured pigment and sealed with wax. By the first century AD, the technique had been adapted so that people could create coloured wax drawings on wooden panels, allowing characters, events and histories to be recorded in vivid colour for the first time. Just like them, the artefacts you're creating today could be pored over by future generations to understand what life right now was like…

DEAR GROWN-UPS

Leaf rubbings are one of the simplest activities we know, requiring few materials and little time to achieve really satisfying results. Like our favourite nature-based activities, it's one that doesn't change much from generation to generation, doesn't need improving, and can be extended any number of ways. Happily, it also doesn't require any special talent or dexterity, so people of all ages can enjoy it equally together. Pack a few crayons in your bag and you'll always have entertainment to hand – no batteries required.

—
1 hour
Autumn
Outdoors or indoors
•• Adult assistance required

Play conkers

For generations, children have been going
nuts for this traditional game of skill.

GATHER TOGETHER
. Conkers (see below)
. String (approximately 30cm
  long per player)
. Notepad and pen for scoring
. Hand drill or skewer
  (to be used by an adult)

LET'S GO!

Step 1. Choose your conkers. Conkers are the seeds of the horse chestnut tree, found inside the knobbly green pods that fall from the branches in autumn (Fig. 1). You'll need several conkers for each. The hardest, strongest conker will win, so you want big, round, shiny ones.

Step 2. Prepare your conkers. Ask an adult to carefully drill a hole through the centre of your conkers, then thread a piece of string through the hole and knot at one end so that the conker can't come off. (N.B. Baking your conker or soaking it in vinegar will harden it, but this is regarded as cheating by conker purists.)

Step 3. Take your positions. Toss a coin to decide which of your two players goes first. To hold your conker, let it dangle

about 20cm from your hand and wrap the excess string around your palm. The striker gets to decide how high they want their opponent to hold the conker.

Step 4. Let battle begin! To take a shot, the striker holds their string in the same way, then draws the conker back with their other hand (Fig. 2). Take aim, and then swing your conker down hard by its string to hit the other player's. The striker gets three shots before players switch roles. If the players' strings get tangled, the first to shout 'snags' gets an extra shot.

Step 5. Keep score. The game is over when one player smashes another's conker (Fig. 3). A conker that hasn't won any battles is called a 'none-er', and one

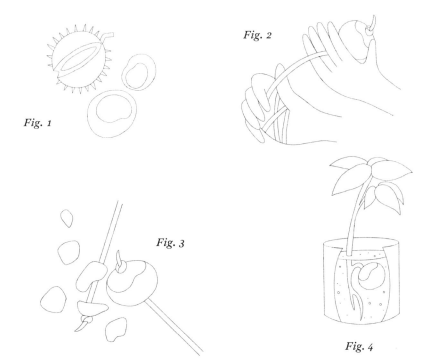

Fig. 1

Fig. 2

Fig. 3

Fig. 4

that's beaten another conker is a 'one-er', graduating to a 'two-er' or 'three-er' if it continues undefeated. However, if your conker wins, it also takes the points from the conker it defeats. So if your 'one-er' smashes another player's 'two-er', your conker becomes a 'three-er'! The player with the highest score wins.

Step 6. Create the next generation of conkers. If you have conkers left over after your tournament, plant them in small pots and cover with 2cm of soil or potting mix (Fig. 4), then leave outdoors until spring, when you should see your saplings begin to sprout!

FROM THE ARCHIVES

The first recorded game of conkers was played on the Isle of Wight in 1848 – and children in Britain have been playing ever since! Some people take it extremely seriously indeed. Every year, the most accomplished players gather in Northamptonshire to get dressed up and take part in the World Conker Championships. With plenty of practice, maybe you'll reign supreme one day...

CREATE THE NEXT GENERATION —
IF YOU HAVE CONKERS LEFT OVER
AFTER YOUR TOURNAMENT, PLANT
THEM AND WAIT UNTIL SPRING!

—

DEAR GROWN-UPS
No wonder the game of conkers has
endured through the generations —
there's the thrill of collecting the perfect
conkers from the woods, the mastery
of the physical skill, and the fun of
competition with friends. There's the
risk of a few rapped knuckles along the
way, of course, but the reward of the
game's enjoyment and lifelong memories
should help to take the sting out!

—
1 hour
All seasons
Indoors and outdoors
•• Adult assistance required

Make your own pinhole camera

Get a new perspective on the world with this simple, satisfying camera.

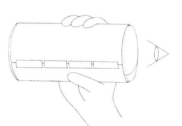

GATHER TOGETHER
. An empty tube of crisps
  (Pringles or similar)
. A sharp pencil or marker pen
. A craft knife (ask an adult
  to help you with this part)
. A drawing pin
. Greaseproof paper
. Glue
. Scissors
. A ruler
. Masking tape
. Aluminium foil

Fig. 1

Fig. 2

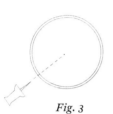

Fig. 3

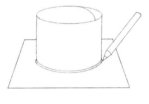

Fig. 4

LET'S GO!

Step 1. Prepare the body of your camera. Give the inside of your tube a thorough clean. Keep the lid as you'll need it in a minute.

Step 2. Mark your tube. About 5cm from the bottom of the tube, draw a line all the way around your cylinder. A good way to keep the line even is to find a small cup or box that's about 5cm tall and, putting it next to your tube, lie your marker or pencil across it so that the tip is just touching the outside of the tube. Don't move the pen – just hold it steady with one hand and rotate the tube with the other – you should get a straight line all the way around (Fig. 1).

Step 3. Cut your tube. Ask an adult to cut all the way around the tube where

you've marked your line using a sharp craft knife (Fig.2).

Step 4. Create your hole. On a camera, the hole that the light enters is called the aperture (which just means 'opening'). Push your drawing pin into the centre of the metal bottom of your tube to make a small hole (Fig. 3).

Step 5. Make your screen. On a piece of greaseproof paper or baking parchment, trace around the edge of your lid and then carefully cut out the circle shape (Fig. 4). Glue the paper circle to the inside of your lid. Put the finished lid on top of the shorter piece of tube (Fig. 5). Stack the longer piece on top and wrap the join with masking tape (Fig. 6).

Fig. 5

Fig. 6

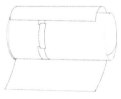

Fig. 7

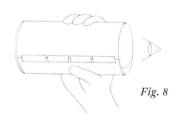

Fig. 8

Step 6. Wrap it well. Take a piece of aluminium foil measuring about 30cm by 20cm, and lie the tube on top so that the bottom lines up with the foil's edge. Roll the foil around the tube slightly and tape down one side. Wrap the whole tube tightly with foil and tape down – you need it to be completely sealed so that no light can enter your tube (Fig. 7). Tuck any overhanging foil into the open end of your tube.

Step 7. Take it for a spin. If it's a sunny day, cup your hands around the end of the tube to prevent light from entering, and look through the open end of your camera – you should see upside-down images on the screen inside (Fig. 8)!

Hold your hand in front of the aperture and move it up and down. The image you see will be doing the reverse! If it's a gloomy day, try it inside – turn a light on in a dimly lit room and stand facing it 1.5 metres away. Drape a blanket over your head to exclude any light from entering. You should see your lamp appear the wrong way up!

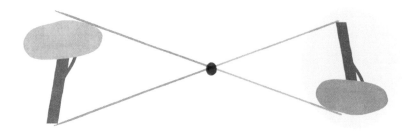

ON A CAMERA, THE HOLE
THAT LIGHT ENTERS THROUGH
IS CALLED THE APERTURE.

FROM THE ARCHIVES

This is the earliest kind of camera, and it's called a 'camera obscura'. They were used in China more than 2,500 years ago, and in 1,000AD an astronomer, Ibn al-Haytham, realised that they could be used to safely view solar eclipses. Ancient cultures feared solar eclipses, but there's nothing dangerous at all about them – provided you never look directly at the sun, which could seriously damage your vision. But with your camera obscura on hand, you're all set!

DEAR GROWN-UPS

The question this activity invariably provokes is 'But why is the image upside down?' So you're ready with a response, it's because light reflects off the surface of the object you're looking at. But it travels in a straight line, so light from the top of an object will pass downwards through the pinhole and to the bottom of the screen, and light from the bottom of the object will travel upwards through the aperture, making the object appear inverted. Now you know!

Go stargazing

Look to the heavens to learn some
amazing astronomy.

GATHER TOGETHER
. Binoculars or a telescope,
  if you have them
. Plenty of warm clothing
. A compass
. A star chart

LET'S GO!
Step 1. Watch the weather. You'll get the
best glimpses of the constellations on
a dry, cold night without clouds – winter
is ideal, but other seasons sometimes
offer perfect viewing conditions too.
You'll be outside, so don't forget to
wrap up very warmly and pack a flask
of something hot to drink.
Step 2. Choose your spot. You might see
a few stars on a cold, bright night in the
city, but the best views are in dark places
where starlight isn't competing with
lights from buildings and streetlights.
Try to get as far from manmade light as
you can for wonderful stargazing.
And aim for a new moon – a full moon
will make it harder to clearly see the
stars. Once you're there, your eyes will

need about 20 minutes to adjust to
the darkness.
Step 3. Look up! Once you're in position,
look skywards. Use your binoculars
or telescope if you have them, but plenty
should be visible to the naked eye.
Can you see:
. *The North Star*: Polaris, or the Pole Star,
is always due north. Look for this one
first – it's bright, and it will help you to
know which direction you're facing.
. *Planets*: Mercury, Venus, Mars, Jupiter
and Saturn should all be visible – they're
all brighter than the stars surrounding
them. Venus shines most brightly.
. *Orion*: This constellation (or grouping
of stars) is usually visible in both the
northern and southern hemispheres

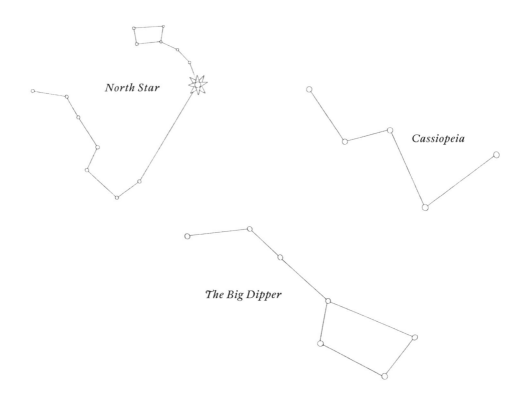

North Star

Cassiopeia

The Big Dipper

because of its position in the skies. It's named after a hunter – look for his belt and sword.

The Big Dipper: Technically not a constellation, but one of the most famous starry sights nonetheless, the Big Dipper consists of four stars forming the 'pot' and three more in a row making the 'handle'. (Sailors have used the Big Dipper for aeons to find their way home.)

Cassiopeia: If you're in the northern hemisphere, look overhead for a giant 'W'.

The Milky Way: One of the most beautiful nighttime views, our own galaxy consists of several hundred billion stars, gas and dust bound together by gravity in a sweeping spiral. It's most visible in summer.

Step 4. Use your star chart (if you have one) to identify as many celestial bodies as you can, or 'collect' them by noting them down in a book once you've observed them.

Step 5. Repeat at different times. The sky is always changing – even on the same night, you'll see different things at different times because the earth is rotating, and as the seasons change and we move in our orbit around the sun, we get different views out to space. You might see meteors in late summer or autumn, a supermoon or a lunar eclipse, depending on the time of year.

IT'S A CHANCE TO WONDER
AT NATURE'S GRANDEUR, TO
CONSIDER THE SCALE OF THINGS,
AND TO BE MOMENTARILY OUT
OF TIME AND PLACE.

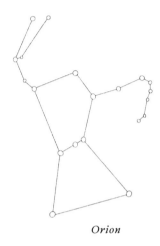

Orion

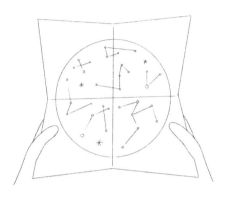

FROM THE ARCHIVES

Looking at the night sky is one thing, but if you wanted to visit some of the sights, how far would you have to travel? If you wanted to get to space, you'd actually only have to drive a car upwards (assuming they worked that way…) for an hour. But if you wanted to see the sun, it would take 20 years to get there flying on a plane. On the way, you'd pass our moon, where you'd still be able to see the footprints of the astronauts who landed there in 1969 – there's no wind on the moon to blow them away!

DEAR GROWN-UPS

Humans have felt a sense of awe when looking skywards since the dawn of time: it's one of the most powerful ways to experience our place in the (much) grander scheme of things. It's a chance to wonder at nature's grandeur, to be absorbed by its beauty, to consider the scale of things, and, maybe most importantly, to be momentarily out of time and place.

DR ANNA LISA VARRI

OCCUPATION
Theoretical astrophysicist

CAREER HIGHLIGHTS
I was just awarded a prize by the Royal Astronomical Society that's named after Caroline Hershel, the first professional female astronomer. She made the very first observations of comets and was the first female to be awarded the gold medal by the RAS, so she's a real role model in this line of research.

How did you become an astronomer?
I was intrigued by mathematics as a child. When people at school explained the Pythagorean theorem, it completely shocked me. For two days I drew triangles on every piece of paper I could find, checking the validity of this statement. I was amazed that it worked each and every time. I realised that there was something in nature that was described by mathematics, that worked irrespective of any conditions, and was giving you an absolute truth.

What does an astronomer actually do?
I do mathematical modelling of stellar systems, which is a small collection of about 10,000 to 100,000 stars. I study their motion and how they behave. An object that I particularly like that's very mathematical in its simplicity is a collection of stars that we call 'globular clusters'. They're beautiful – they're like jewels in the sky and because they are relatively close to us we can observe them in detail. I tend to do a mixture of pen-and-paper calculations (I'm a bit old fashioned!) and simulations on computers. I work in an office – I've been to a mountaintop observatory just once. It's not a normal thing for a theoretical physicist to do because we are essentially useless up on a mountain! The observational astronomers were very kind and took me along once… but most of the time I'm in a university.

How often do you make new discoveries in your line of work?
There are two classes of discovery: theoretical and observational. In the first category, a 'discovery' is the moment you have a complete theory that can account for an open problem. Maybe twice in my career so far I've had this kind of moment. It's fantastic! And then there's a discovery in the observational sense, where you receive data that reveals a new astronomical object, galaxy or small galaxies that were previously unknown, or strings of stars in remote parts of the Milky Way. The feeling of discovery is the same – the fantastic moment when you realise that you are the first person on earth to see something new, or to make a discovery that didn't exist before.

What's your favourite thing to see in the sky?
I have a lifelong appreciation of Cassiopeia (see 'Stargazing' activity). I always look for it in the night sky and find peace in seeing it in different parts of the northern hemisphere. Also, knowing that anything we see in the night sky has a time delay. The light that we see from the sun takes eight minutes to get to us. The light of faraway galaxies is much older because they are so far away – it takes millions of years to get to us. The sky is really a time machine. It's incredible.

—
2 hours
All seasons
Outdoors and indoors
•• **Adult assistance required**

Map your neighbourhood

Share your secret neighbourhood knowledge in your own personal map.

GATHER TOGETHER
. Paper
. Coloured pens and pencils
. Eraser
. A compass

LET'S GO!

Step 1. Choose your area. Ever since humans started exploring the world, maps have been used to share information about where to find food, or populations, or buried treasure, or dangers to avoid. Decide what kind of map you'd like to make: a helpful guide of the best local places to play? An imaginary map of where your cat likes to go each day? A map plotting where each of your friends lives nearby?

Step 2. Go on a reconnaissance mission (that's what it's called when an army sends out a small advance team to research the area). Take a walk around your neighbourhood looking for the kinds of things you've decided to map out. Note or sketch them on your notepad to remind you once you've got home. You might like to use a compass to work out which way you're facing, so you'll know where to put the features on your map. To do this, make sure the red needle lines up with the 'N' – that's pointing towards due north. The compass face will tell you which way you're facing.

Step 3. Sketch out your map. With light pencil strokes, plan out where everything will go: buildings, playgrounds, local cats, schools, train stations... Think about how much distance there is between things, and how big certain things are – in other words, the scale of your map. You might need to redraw a few times to get it right.

ONE PLACE MAY BE MAPPED
OVER AND OVER AGAIN,
AND BE COMPLETELY
DIFFERENT EACH TIME.

Step 4. Add detail. Colour in your map, adding details such as leaves on trees, cars, people – whatever helps your map to look like the picture you have of your neighbourhood in your mind.

Step 5. Label your map. Write small tags alongside important features: Silas's house, the library, best pizza place... it will help the reader to immediately find places of interest.

Step 6. Add a key. This is a panel on the side of your map that explains any information needed to read it, such as scale, or symbols you've used. Add a compass so people know which way to go.

Step 7. Go exploring! Retrace your route with a friend – can they find their way around using only your map as a guide?

FROM THE ARCHIVES

Maps (and their makers) are incredibly powerful. America is named after a mapmaker, Amerigo Vespucci. A cholera outbreak in mid-19th-century London was halted when the cases were mapped, helping to isolate the source (a single water pump). During World War II, American and British soldiers carried special sets of playing cards that, if soaked, revealed secret maps to help them escape. The completely made-up city of El Dorado drove generations of explorers to distraction as they tried to locate it, thanks to erroneous maps. Even in our age of Google Maps, there are still plenty of discoveries to be made, and recorded, on maps. And, as your map shows, there are as many possible maps as there are people. What might an owl's map of your neighbourhood look like? An ant's? Or a Martian's? One place may be mapped over and over again, and be completely different each time.

—

DEAR GROWN-UPS

Children adore maps – they're a way of learning about their place in the world, and of dreaming about what lies beyond their familiar locales. But far beyond simple geography, when you allow your child to lead this activity, you'll actually see the beauty, poetry, mystery and magic of your neighbourhood through their eyes. Mapmaking is a way of laying claim to a part of the world, and is a wonderful way of developing your child's sense of place and belonging, as well as their powers of observation.

Winter

EAT
Clementines *(citrus x clementina)*
. Are a hybrid of sweet oranges and
  mandarin oranges.
. Are named after the Algerian monk,
  Brother Marie-Clément, in whose
  garden the fruit first spontaneously
  appeared.
. Are nicknamed the 'Christmas orange'
  as they're available from November
  to January.
. Contain an oil which can help you sleep
  better, worry less and feel happier.

DO
Feed birds
Short days (so less time to hunt), bitter
cold to endure and less plentiful food
mean birds need all the help they can
get in the coldest months.
. Set up a feeder, high up off the ground
  away from predators
. Leave out high-fat foods once a day
. Scraps such as cooked fat or meat,
  vegetables, pastry, biscuits or dried
  fruit are perfect
. Only leave out as much as gets eaten
  each day (any more will attract pests)
. Never give them salty foods – it will
  make them ill!

LOOK

Sun dogs

A sun dog (or parhelion, as it's properly known) is an atmospheric optical phenomenon where a bright spot is visible on one or both sides of the sun.

They occur when light is refracted from hexagonal ice crystals suspended in high clouds. And although sun isn't necessarily something you associate with winter, its lower position in the sky makes winter the best time to spot them.

READ

. *The Night Before Christmas* by Clement Clark Moore
. *The Snowy Day* by Ezra Jack Keats
. *The Quiet Music of Gently Falling Snow* by Jackie Morris

PICTURE-BOOKS IN WINTER

Summer fading, winter comes—
Frosty mornings, tingling thumbs
Window robins, winter rooks,
And the picture story-books.

Water now is turned to stone
Nurse and I can walk upon;
Still we find the flowing brooks
In the picture story-books.

All the pretty things put by,
Wait upon the children's eye,
Sheep and shepherds, trees and crooks,
In the picture story-books.

We may see how all things are,
Seas and cities, near and far,
And the flying fairies' looks,
In the picture story-books.

How am I to sing your praise,
Happy chimney-corner days,
Sitting safe in nursery nooks,
Reading picture story-books?

— Robert Louis Stevenson

ALFAJORES

These buttery biscuits are traditionally eaten around Christmas time in Spain and parts of Latin America — but they're absolutely delicious any time of year.

75 MINS PREP
8 TO 10 MINS COOKING

INGREDIENTS
300g plain flour
200g butter
1 egg
100g sugar
Dulce de leche

Put the plain flour in a bowl and make a small hole in the centre.

Add your room-temperature butter, egg and sugar to the bowl in the hole you've made. Use a fork and light mixing movements to gently combine the ingredients into a soft dough.

Rest dough in the fridge for two hours. On a flour-sprinkled table, use a rolling pin dusted with flour to gently roll the dough out as thinly as possible.

Use a small glass to press out rounds of your dough and place on a baking tray. Cook them in an oven at 175°C for 8 minutes or until dark beige.

Allow to cool and then sandwich two together with dulce de leche.

Build your own marble run

Rig up an obstacle course and balls away!

GATHER TOGETHER
. A big cardboard box
. Cardboard tubes (from inside wrapping paper, kitchen roll, cling film etc)
. Scrap cardboard (cereal boxes and that kind of thing)
. Newspaper to roll into tubes
. Plastic bottles
. Sticky tape
. Glue
. Blu Tack
. Scissors
. Paper cup
. Marbles
. Any extra 'features' you'd like to add, like funnels, old pinwheel toys, or things to decorate with

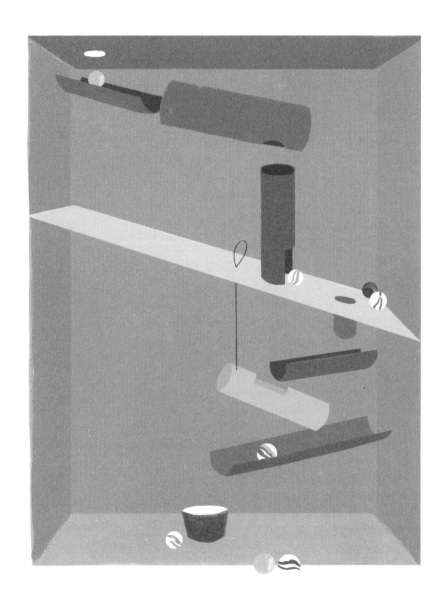

WHOSE MARBLE IS FASTEST?
DO DIFFERENT-SIZED MARBLES
GO FASTER OR SLOWER?
CAN YOU MAKE IT EVEN MORE
COMPLICATED?

LET'S GO!

Step 1. Cut out your frame. Cut one side off the biggest cardboard box you can find (Fig. 1). This will become the frame for your marble run so you want as much room as possible to work with.

Step 2. Make an opening. With your box on its end and the open side facing outwards, cut a small hole in the top where you'll drop in your marble (Fig. 2).

Step 3. Build your run. Create the course your marble will run along using the items you've plundered from your recycling box. You want it to have as many twists and turns as possible. Generally, you'll use tubes to carry your marble across each level, and holes, funnels or bends to turn corners and drop down to the next level.

Starting below your hole, tape or glue a cardboard tube across your box (angled downwards so that gravity helps your marble along), making sure there's a hole in the tube below your entry point. At the end of your first tube, create a connection (cut a hole in the bottom at the end of the tube, or tape rolled-up newspaper or curved cardboard to the end of your tube) so the marble can drop down to the tube below (Fig. 3).

Step 4. Add extras. Cut the top off a plastic bottle and use it upside down to drop a marble down a level. Cut holes along the bottom of a tube – will the marble drop out at a different point if it's going faster or slower? Experiment and see. Use plenty of tape or glue as you go.

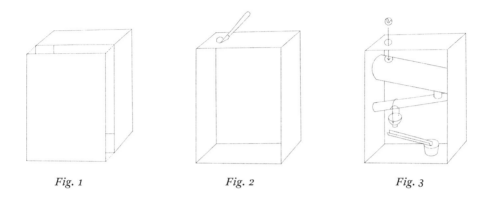

Fig. 1   Fig. 2   Fig. 3

Step 5. Keep building until you reach the bottom. Test your run occasionally as you add to it – if you want your marble to go faster, angle the tubes downwards. If you want to slow it down, tilt the tubes up, or add obstacles to your course. Make it as complicated as you like.
Step 6. Add a small cup at the very end of your run to catch your marbles in.
Step 7. Ready, steady, go! Drop a marble through your hole at the top to send it down your run. Whose marble is fastest? Do different-sized marbles go faster or slower? Can you make it even more complicated? (Advanced marble-runners can create several different tube endings for the marble to go down, with points for which tube it finally comes out of.)

FROM THE ARCHIVES
Can you imagine how much fun a mega marble run would be? That's just what a team in Flumserberg, Switzerland created when they built the world's longest marble run, measuring an incredible 2,858.9 metres long! If you train to become a marble run maestro, you might one day snatch that record yourself...

BUILD YOUR OWN MARBLE RUN

FOR BUDDING ENGINEERS, A
MARBLE RUN IS THE ULTIMATE
PLAYGROUND.

—

DEAR GROWN-UPS

For budding engineers, a marble run is
the ultimate playground. As an open-
ended activity it presents plenty of scope
for creativity and ingenuity to direct
the outcome, and the three-dimensional
nature of the task gently develops
understandings of gravity, momentum
and spatial reasoning. It's not an easy
activity, nor one that offers instant
gratification, so there's an opportunity
to foster patience and problem-solving
in tackling this one, too.

—
3 hours
Autumn and winter
Indoors and outdoors
•• Adult assistance required

Freeze ice baubles

Make your own magical disappearing
baubles on an ice-cold day.

GATHER TOGETHER

. Some string
. Scissors
. A muffin tray
. A jug of water
. Decorations (almost anything can go inside, depending on who you're making them for! You could use lovely leaves or flowers, or birdseed for your feathered friends, berries for a sibling or even a rolled-up secret message for a friend to unfurl once it's thawed.)

LET'S GO!

Step 1. Prepare your string hangers. Cut short lengths of string (with an adult's help) and tie the ends together to create a loop. Place the knotted end of one loop in each cup of the muffin tray.

Step 2. Add your decorations. Put your chosen decorations in each cup of the muffin tray.

Step 3. Add water. Fill each cup ⅔ full with water from your jug. If the string pops out, tuck it under your decorations to anchor it.

Step 4. Put the tray in the freezer until your baubles are frozen solid.

Step 5. String them up. Run a little warm water over the bottom of the muffin tray to release the baubles, and quickly pack them to string up outside.

You could hang them outside your windows, on friends' doorknobs for them to find, dangle seed-filled baubles from the branches of trees as a treat for the local birds, or string them around the neighbourhood from railings for people to wonder at as they pass by.

FROM THE ARCHIVES

Igloos – structures built completely from bricks of ice and snow – can be up to 37°C warmer inside than the temperature outside. This is because ice, although freezing cold, is a very good insulator, so traps the body heat of the inhabitants inside.

—

DEAR GROWN-UPS

Getting outdoors in winter can be unappealing, to say the least, but there's just as much to be gained and discovered from a chilly day out. This activity involves two separate excursions – one to collect materials, and one to deliver the finished baubles. It's a wonderful way to mark the winter solstice, Christmas or perihelion (for extra trivia points...). Just bundle up, pack some hot cocoa, and embrace the elements.

Create an advent calendar

Count down the days to Christmas with your own advent calendar.

LET'S GO!

Step 1. Number your envelopes from 1 to 25.

Step 2. Each of your notecards will contain an idea for a task or activity — but first you need to decide who your advent calendar is for. Will your family share one, taking it in turns to open the envelopes? You'll need to think of activities the whole family can do. Is it for a friend? You could think of things you know they will especially enjoy. Or will it contain ideas for good deeds you could do in the lead-up to Christmas? Here are some ideas for tasks:

. Make a bird feeder to help birds through the winter.
. Donate an item to your local food bank or shelter.
. Take breakfast in bed to your parents.
. Make popcorn and watch a special Christmas film together.
. Go ice-skating with friends.
. Go for a starry walk on a clear winter's night.
. Decorate paper for wrapping Christmas presents.
. Make mulled apple juice and mince pies.
. Come up with your own ideas (or look elsewhere in this book for inspiration) Write one activity on each piece of paper and slip it inside an envelope. (Hint: you might want to make Christmas Day itself something simple as the day tends to be busy.) Add a small chocolate or sweet to each envelope and seal.

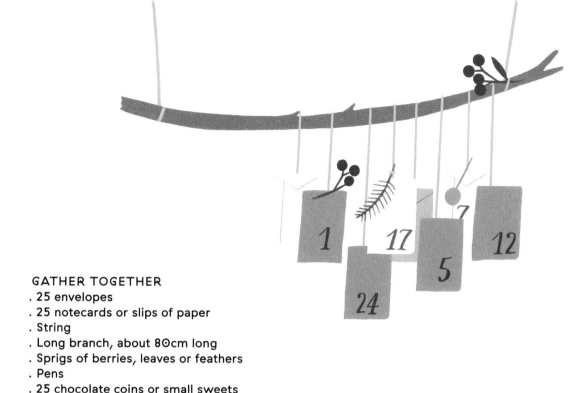

GATHER TOGETHER
. 25 envelopes
. 25 notecards or slips of paper
. String
. Long branch, about 80cm long
. Sprigs of berries, leaves or feathers
. Pens
. 25 chocolate coins or small sweets

Step 3. Construct your calendar. Use a hole punch (a kitchen skewer will work too) to make a small hole in the top corner of each envelope. Thread through a long piece of string and tie a knot in one end so that the envelope won't slide off the string. Tie the other end to your branch so it dangles down. Space the envelopes (from 1 to 25) along the length of the branch, using different lengths of string so they hang at different heights.
Step 4. Decorate your calendar by tying strings to clusters of berries, sprigs of greenery or feathers and tying them to the branch among the envelopes until it looks nice. You could twist some string lights along the branch if you have them.

Step 5. Tie a long piece of string (say 1 metre) to either end of the branch and hang your calendar from a small tack on the wall.
Step 6. Each day, open the envelope corresponding to that day's date and enjoy both the treat and the task.

FROM THE ARCHIVES

The word 'advent' comes from the Latin *adventus*, meaning 'arrival'. It was originally a season of fasting and quiet contemplation, but we prefer the kind that involves foil-wrapped chocolates! Not all advent calendars are made of paper; some are simply special candles that are burned down day by day. Making your own advent calendar, as well as being a clever way to sneak daily chocolate in with your parents' approval, is a great way to pack December full of fun, instead of just waiting for Christmas Day itself.

DEAR GROWN-UPS

In a world of instant gratification, the run-up to Christmas presents an opportunity to practise (and model) patience. It's an essential skill for children to acquire, and an advent calendar helps to cultivate that self-control as well as focusing attention on the less materialistic aspects of the season. Try an altruistic calendar, or an entirely nature-focused edition, to help slow down and ground your family at this most wonderful (and hectic) time of year.

Wrap your gifts

Make your presents too lovely
to unwrap – almost!

GATHER TOGETHER

. Gifts to wrap
. Fabric squares (clean napkins or linen
  tea towels will do, or cut similarly sized
  squares from fabric scraps)
. Potato
. Craft knife (and an adult to use it...)
. Acrylic or fabric paint
. Shallow dish
. Craft or butcher's paper
. Scissors
. Sticky tape
. Ribbon or string

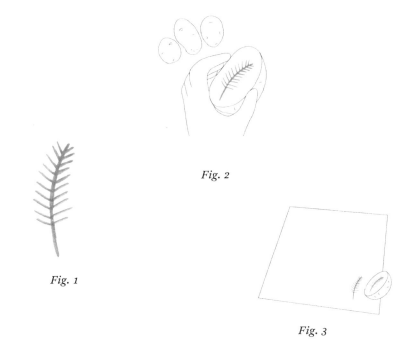

Fig. 2

Fig. 1

Fig. 3

LET'S GO!

Step 1. Choose your wrapping material. The Japanese tradition of presenting gifts wrapped in fabric is called *furoshiki*, and gives the recipient two gifts – the beautiful fabric used for wrapping and the thoughtful present inside. Paper is another sustainable alternative to non-recyclable shop-bought papers.

Step 2. Decorate your wrapping material. Choose a simple shape to print – a Christmas tree, feather or sprig of leaves (Fig. 1) are pretty, but spots, lighting bolts, stars or letters will also look lovely. Ask an adult to cut a potato in half and use the tip of the craft knife to mark out your shape (Fig. 2). Using horizontal cuts, remove the potato around the shape you want to print to a depth of 50mm. Put some paint in a dish then dip your potato stamp in it. Stamp firmly across your paper or fabric to create your pattern (Fig. 3). Allow it to dry completely.

Step 3. Wrap your gift, using your fabric (see Fig. 4 and Fig. 5 for techniques for wrapping different shapes) or paper.

Step 4. Add finishing touches. When you tie your parcel with string or ribbon, tuck in a simple sprig of lavender, spruce or fern, or tie on a slice of dried citrus or rosemary for seasonal fragrance.

THE JAPANESE TRADITION OF
PRESENTING GIFTS WRAPPED
IN FABRIC IS CALLED FUROSHIKI.

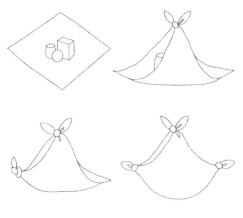

Fig. 4

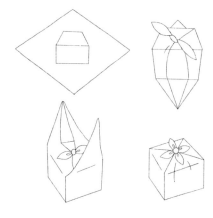

Fig. 5

FROM THE ARCHIVES

In Japanese culture, how a gift is wrapped is as important as the gift itself. It's called *tsutsumu*, and careful presentation is a way of demonstrating your respect for the recipient – in fact, giving an unwrapped or badly wrapped gift is considered pretty rude. But learning to wrap something beautifully (and sustainably, if you use fabric which can be reused) will make even the humblest offering seem truly special. In Japan, people even take care to carefully tie up their lunchbox in *furoshiki* – making unwrapping even the most ordinary lunch quite a special occasion!

DEAR GROWN-UPS

Gift-giving can get wrapped up (if you'll pardon the pun...) with consumerist culture, but thinking about, and practising, the art of wrapping the Japanese way prompts children to remember why we give gifts: as a token of our feelings for another person. It's a reminder, especially during the Christmas season, that the simplest gifts given thoughtfully are the ones we cherish the most.

WRAP YOUR GIFTS

Make a snowman

Make the most of a snow day by building
the coolest new friend.

GATHER TOGETHER
. Appropriate clothing for yourself
  (hat, waterproof gloves and boots
  as well as your usual winter layers)
. Materials to adorn your snowman —
  buttons or stones for eyes, a carrot
  for a nose and a hat or scarf are
  traditional, but be guided by your
  own imagination

LET'S GO!

Step 1. Find the perfect snow. It should be around -1°C, which is not too cold (it will be too powdery to build with) and not too warm and wet (too sloppy). To test it out, pick up a few handfuls and pack it into a ball. If it stays together, you've got good snow! You'll need to find a spot with plenty of it, too, since a tall snowman needs up to 19 cubic feet of snow.

Step 2. Make a big snowball in your hands, then roll it along the ground. It will pick up snow as you roll it. Every now and then, stop rolling and use your hands to pack it together well.

Step 3. When your ball is as big as you want the base to be, roll it to a flat spot where it will stand, and pack extra snow around the bottom to hold it in place.

Step 4. Make another ball to go on top, following step 2. Make this one about two thirds the size of the first one. It will be quite heavy, so roll it over to the base of your snowman. Flatten the top of the first snowball to give the second one a stable place to sit. With friends or an adult, lift the second ball and carefully place it on right in the centre of the first one. Pack some snow around the join to secure it.

Step 5. Make your snowman's head, following step 2. Make this one about two thirds the size of the second one, rolling it over to the snowman when you're happy with it. Flatten the top of the second snowball, and carefully (with friends' or an adult's help) place

CONTRARY TO A POPULAR
AND ENDURING MYTH, SOME
SNOWFLAKES DO SHARE
THE SAME STRUCTURE.

your head on top. Pack some more snow around the 'neck' where the two balls meet to keep it in place.

Step 6. Decorate your snowman. Is it a man, a woman, or even an animal? Is it friendly or funny-looking? Is it modelled after someone you know? You could poke some sticks into its body as arms, or use leaves for hair. Give it a face, using pebbles or bouncy balls or buttons for eyes, a carrot or banana for a nose, or a string of pebbles or raisins for a mouth.

Step 7. Dress your snowman. Use old items of clothing (nothing that will be missed!) to dress him up. Is he heading off to work? Is she on holiday somewhere exotic? Old glasses, sun hats, scarves and shirts offer plenty of possibilities.

FROM THE ARCHIVES

The first ever photograph of a snowflake was taken by a farmer in Jericho, Vermont in the United States. For years, Wilson Bentley tried to connect microscopes to an early kind of camera, before he finally succeeded in 1885. For the rest of his life, his obsession continued, photographing more than 5,000 individual, completely unique snowflakes. But – contrary to an extremely popular and enduring myth – some snowflakes do share the same structure. In 1988, during a storm in Wisconsin, a scientist found two identical snow crystals, finally debunking the idea.

DEAR GROWN-UPS

Bundling up and getting outdoors has benefits far and above just getting some fresh air (although it certainly helps to avoid the winter germs!). Building a snowman uses large, infrequently used muscles and gross motor skills, in a season where such opportunities are hard to come by. Navigating the strange, challenging icy environment offers a chance for children to flex problem-solving abilities, presenting them with physical and creative challenges to solve. And bolstering vitamin D exposure will help to keep wintertime spirits high long after the snow has thawed, too.

Send a secret message

Spy-approved techniques for
top secret missions.

GATHER TOGETHER
. Paper
. Two pencils
. Sticky tape
. Cotton bud
. Lemon juice
. Banana
. Toothpick
. White crayon
. Felt–tip markers

LET'S GO!
Codes and secret messages are excellent ways to send sneaky messages for your friends' eyes only. There are lots of different methods, but here are four to try. Remember, you'll need to make sure the person receiving the message knows how to reveal it.

Scytale
The ancient Romans used to send top secret missives this way, writing their information down on paper wrapped tightly around a cylinder. We're going to use pencils – the result is just as cryptic. You and a friend need to have matching pencils for this method. Take a thin strip of paper, maybe 0.5cm wide and 30cm long, and tape one end to the very top of your pencil. Wrap the strip very tightly around your pencil, lining it up as you go so that there are no gaps showing, all the way to the bottom. When you've wrapped your entire pencil, use a small piece of tape to secure the bottom end of your paper strip.

Use a sharp pencil or pen to write your message neatly in small letters lengthwise down the barrel of your pencil, just like you're writing a letter (Fig. 1). When you've finished, peel up the tape at both ends and unravel your paper from the pencil. You can now see letters on it, but you can't read it! To read the message, all your friend has to do is rewrap their matching pencil with the strip, and your message is right there again.

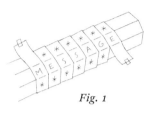

Fig. 1

Fig. 3

Fig. 2

Fig. 4

Invisible ink

Take a sheet of paper, some lemon juice squeezed into a cup, and a cotton bud. Dip your cotton bud in the lemon juice and use the wet tip like you would pencil to write your message (Fig. 2). Keep moistening the tip to make sure you're leaving a lemony trace. As it dries, it will disappear. When you give it to your friend it will look like any blank sheet of paper – but when they hold the paper under a lamp bulb, your message will appear like magic.

Banananote

Here's the perfect way to pass on a secret message at school – anyone who intercepts it will just see a perfectly normal banana! Use a toothpick to gently mark your message on the banana's skin. (Fig. 3) Right now, it just looks like an ordinary banana, but in an hour's time, the writing will darken so your friend can read it.

White-out

Write your message using a white wax crayon on a sheet of unlined white paper. It's hard to read, until your friend, who knows there's a message to be revealed, colours all over the page with a felt-tip marker. There it is, your secret message!

PEOPLE HAVE BEEN WRITING
SECRET MESSAGES FOR AS LONG AS
THEY'VE BEEN WRITING AT ALL.

FROM THE ARCHIVES

People have been writing secret messages as long as they've been writing at all. It's serious stuff – in World War II, the Allies' ability to break German codes enabled them to out-strategise the Nazis and is estimated to have shortened the war by two years. On Easter Island, just as mysterious as the Rapa Nui people's huge stone heads is their secret writing system called 'rongorongo'. This system of glyphs, carefully carved into wooden tablets, has never been deciphered, keeping the Rapa Nui's secrets very safe indeed.

DEAR GROWN-UPS

The thrill of a secret is a childhood delight – in a world over which they have little control, a secret belongs to them. It's a tiny taste of independence from adult oversight, and creates a really powerful sense of autonomy and privacy that helps encourage development of their inner world and imagination. By their nature, secrets exclude some but include others – so as a tool or currency of friendship, they can be used to build meaningful bonds, too.

ANNA GRAM

OCCUPATION
Spy

CAREER HIGHLIGHTS
I'm afraid that's classified.

How did you become a spy?

When I was a child, I was always very nosy, desperate to find out what people didn't want me to find out. When I was at school I realised I loved finding clues and patterns and, in particular, working out what it was that made people tick. When I was leaving university, thinking about what to do as a job, some clever advertising piqued my nosiness, and inspired me to use my interests to help protect the country and, in turn, those people I care about. When I started work, I got to learn the tricks of the trade, and to work out how to turn doing what I enjoyed into a useful job.

What do spies really do?

The job of a spy is to gather the data and information that our adversaries don't want us to know about, which, if used correctly, can help to keep people safe. Really good spies can get this intelligence without the targets ever knowing how and when it was taken. Spies never work alone. They are part of a big team, full of different people with different roles. Intelligence analysts are based at headquarters and analyse all the different types of intelligence that comes in from all the different sources and piece it together. But of course, they need other spies 'on the ground' who can get the intelligence for them. So really, it's a massive team job.

Do spies really get to use amazing secret agent gadgets? What's your favourite? Or is there one you'd like to invent?
Yes! They really do. The spy world is at the cutting edge of technology and it needs to constantly be ahead of the game. They always need new inventors to help design stealthier tools to help capture intelligence and get it securely back to headquarters. The best gadgets look like normal everyday household items – and I don't just mean pens and watches. Look around your house and garden and think about the craziest item that could be used to somehow capture information... and I bet that the intelligence industry is already working out how.

How can you tell if someone's a spy?
If you can tell that someone is a spy, they're doing a really bad job and their cover is blown. The best spies blend in, melt into the background and are forgotten the moment they're seen.

What is your essential spy equipment?
The most basic equipment you need is yourself: your ears, eyes and brain. You already have all the tools you need to become a spy. You just have to be clever in how you use them.

What's the riskiest thing you've done?
The biggest risk is acting alone. It's essential to keep yourself and others safe, and to not take dangerous risks.

INTERVIEW

Memory game

How sharp is your memory?
Let's find out...

GATHER TOGETHER
. Up to 15 objects collected from nature
. Basket for carrying your finds
. White sheet of paper or fabric
. Fabric to use as a blindfold

LET'S GO!
Step 1. Collect your objects. Head outside and pick up 15 items you find in your garden, neighbourhood or park. Look for a good mix of textures, like feathers, petals, pebbles, sticks, nuts, leaves or fronds.

Step 2. Lay the objects out on a white sheet and give the other person a minute to memorise them. For younger children, make it easier by only presenting them with 5 objects, while older players can manage more.

Step 3. Blindfold the player (or players) doing the memorising, and take one of the objects away. With their blindfold removed, ask them to guess which one is missing. The correct guesser wins a point. Put the object back and repeat, this time taking a different item away. The first player to reach an agreed score is the winner.

Step 4. Try some variations. If you've got a group of people, lay the objects out and give the players 1 or 2 minutes to memorise the objects on display. Then hide them all out of sight and ask the players to write down as many as they can remember within an agreed time limit. The person who remembers most is the winner! Or play a 'touch' version – follow the same steps as before, but instead of taking the blindfold off, ask them to work out which item has been taken away by touching the remaining objects on the sheet.

FROM THE ARCHIVES

Despite how often you might find yourself forgetting to bring your sports kit to school, your memory is actually capable of staggering feats of learning and retaining knowledge. One expert, Professor Paul Reber of Northwestern University, roughly calculates that the human brain can store 2.5 petabytes of data – equivalent to 2.5 MILLION GIGABYTES. There goes your excuse for not finishing your homework.

DEAR GROWN-UPS

The memory game is as satisfying to play as it is simple. This challenging but straightforward game gives the brain a real workout, boosting concentration and attention to detail, improving vocabulary, training the visual and short-term memory and fostering the ability to classify different objects. It's surprisingly addictive for adults, too – and confers the same benefits!

Shadow animals

Conjure your own menagerie from thin air!

GATHER TOGETHER
. A lamp — with a bendy neck so you can angle it correctly or a shade you can remove
. A white sheet or bare white wall

LET'S GO!

Step 1. Set the stage. You'll need a dark room so that you can see your light clearly on the wall, and an area of unobstructed white wall.

Step 2. Position your light. You make shadows by putting an object between a light and another surface: in this case, you'll be putting your hands between your light and the wall you want to cast your shadow animals on. Remove the lampshade and angle your light so that the strongest light is aimed at the wall.

Step 3. Make your menagerie. Practise bending your fingers into the shapes shown below for each animal.

Step 4. Bring them to life. Once you've got your hands in position, try adding small movements to animate them – perhaps an ear cocking or a nose twitching, or even scampering across your screen.

Step 5. Keep practising! Perhaps you could team up with a friend or sibling to act out a story, with shadow animals in the starring roles...

Wolf

Rabbit

Dove

Dog

FROM THE ARCHIVES

Your shadow is a magical thing because, unlike the body it's connected to, it changes size depending on the time of day. That's because your shadow is created by light being blocked from reaching the ground by your body. So in the middle of the day, when the sun is directly overhead, you won't see your shadow because light is able to fall onto the floor around you. But in the early morning and afternoon, when the sun is much lower in the sky, the light hits your sides, so your body blocks much more of the light and your shadow appears much longer. It's also longer in winter than in summer – do you know why...?

DEAR GROWN-UPS

Shadow animals fall into the wonderful category of games that require next to no special equipment other than imagination. The finger positions require patience to master as well as fine motor skills, and animating them fosters imagination and empathy with creatures large and small.

Plant a terrarium

How does your garden grow?
In a bottle, that's how!

GATHER TOGETHER
. A large, clear glass bottle or jar, ideally one with a wide mouth
. Several handfuls of gravel or pebbles
. Several handfuls of soil
. A small plant or two (you can buy a small succulent, or carefully dig up a little plant with its roots from your garden)
. A long stick — a chopstick, long-handled spoon or pencil will all work well
. Decorative items like moss, figurines, shells or pebbles
. A jug or small watering can

LET'S GO!
Step 1. Prepare your bottle. Wash it thoroughly with warm soapy water inside and out, rinse and dry it. This will make sure enough light can reach the plants and will get rid of any bacteria that could damage them.

Step 2. Add your layers. First of all, drop your gravel or pebbles into the bottom of the jar. This will help drain moisture away from the roots. Next, moisten your soil: you don't want it to be wet, just slightly damp, so a spray from a water bottle should do the trick. Put a layer of soil twice as thick as your layer of stones into the container, and use your stick to tamp it down and stop it sticking to the bottle's sides.

Step 3. Using your stick, create a small hole where you want your plant (or plants) to go. Gently lower them in, roots first, then use your fingers or long stick to carefully cover the roots with soil.

Step 4. Add your decorative objects to the jar. A layer of moss or lichen looks lovely and helps to keep the soil moist. You could use small figurines to create playful scenes, or shells for an underwater effect... whatever stirs your imagination!

Step 5. Water your garden. This is *very important* to get right. Too much water and your garden will rot, and too little water and it will shrivel up. Your garden will only need a dribble of water every month or so – just enough to keep the

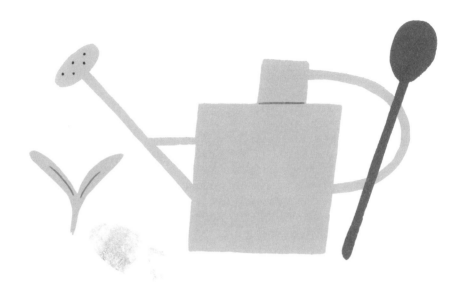

soil moist. To water it, carefully use your jug or watering can spout to trickle water down the inside of the bottle as you slowly rotate it, so that you water a tiny bit all the way around it. This will help to keep the glass clean, too. Position it somewhere fairly sunny indoors. That's it. You're a micro-gardener!

FROM THE ARCHIVES
Terrariums (sometimes called 'bottle gardens') are closed environments that are self-sustaining (they don't need anything from outside in order to function). This kind of environment is called an ecosystem. Our world is actually a kind of terrarium – the soil is the earth, the plants are our forests, the water supply is like our oceans. In your terrarium, like on earth, water evaporates from the ground and then condenses again into droplets that fall back to quench the soil. So you're not just a gardener – you've created a world!

OUR WORLD IS ACTUALLY A KIND
OF TERRARIUM — THE SOIL IS OUR
EARTH, THE PLANTS ARE FORESTS,
AND THE WATER SUPPLY IS OUR
OCEANS.

—

DEAR GROWN-UPS
If you want to help a child feel godlike,
let them create their own world
in a bottle! As well as the creative
satisfaction of putting it together,
it offers a chance to practise very
manageable gardening skills —
terrariums are fairly forgiving. The
finished product helps to purify and
humidify the air, too, so it's a low-
responsibility, low-effort project that
pays high dividends all round.

From 10 minutes to 1 hour
All seasons
Indoors

Rainy day games

Playing these fun games is the silver lining
to having the wintertime sniffles.

LET'S GO!
Fortune Teller
For at least two players
Step 1. Make your fortune teller:
. Fold a square sheet of paper (at least 20cm x 20cm) into quarters and unfold again.
. Fold each of the four corners into the paper's centre point.
. Turn your folded paper over and fold each of the four corners into the paper's centre point on this side.
. Fold the paper into quarters again.
. Fit your fingers into the pockets underneath and pinch the tips together to make a closed 'beak'. This is your fortune teller!
. Colour each of the four outermost surfaces in a different colour. Label the inner surfaces from one to eight. Beneath each of the eight inner surfaces, write an inventive 'fortune' (think of some funny or thrilling things that could happen to someone – the more adventurous, the better!).

Step 2. Tell someone's fortune:
. Ask someone to pick from the colours on the outside of your fortune teller.
. Spell out the colour as you open and close the fortune teller – for 'red', for example, open and close it three times.
. Ask them to choose a number from inside the fortune teller where it's stopped.
. Count that number aloud as you open and close the fortune teller that many times.

BEING STUCK IN BED WITH A COLD
CAN BE BORING — BUT YOU COULD
ALSO HAVE A BREAKTHROUGH...

. Ask the person to choose a new number
from the options revealed inside.
. Open the flap and read the fortune
hidden below the number they
have chosen!

Constantinople
For as many players as you like
Step 1. Choose a long word (like
'Constantinople'!). Have your pens
and paper at the ready.
Step 2. Write down as many words
as you can using those letters. Set the
timer for 2 minutes, and when it goes off,
whoever has written the most words is
the winner!

Picture Perfect
For at least two players
Step 1. Create your clues. Each player
writes five clues on separate scraps of
paper and then folds them up and puts
them in a central bowl. (Clues could be
the name of a book, a famous person's
name, or a common phrase.)
Step 2. Nominate a drawer. That person
picks a clue from the bowl and then has
one minute to to get the other players to
correctly guess what it is by drawing it —
without using letters or numbers!
Step 3. Keep score. The artist and the
person who guessed correctly both get a
point. The person on the left of the artist
is the next person to choose and draw.
Whoever ends with most points wins.

FROM THE ARCHIVES

Being stuck in bed with a cold can be boring – but as well as getting some rest, you could also have a breakthrough. Paul McCartney from The Beatles dreamt the now-famous melody for 'Yesterday' and was convinced it must be someone else's song as it sounded so familiar – as it now does to millions of his fans! The Periodic Table came to its inventor, Dmitry Mendeleyev, while he slept, and scientist Dr James Watson had a dream of a double helix shape that solved the conundrum of the shape of our DNA. So rest easy – great things can happen while you doze.

DEAR GROWN-UPS

Children's lives can be every bit as hectic as adults', so when minor illnesses strike it can be an opportunity for both patient and carer to slow down a little. Gentle games, classic films, comforting food and one-on-one time with a parent might be just what the doctor ordered – for both of you.

Play a game of elastics

Hours of fun is just a hop, a skip
and a jump away.

GATHER TOGETHER
. 2 metres of narrow braided elastic
. Two dining chairs (if playing alone)
. Two friends (if playing in a group)

LET'S GO!
Step 1. Make your elastics. Tie the ends of a 2-metre piece of elastic together in a double knot to make a loop.
Step 2. Make a frame. If you're playing by yourself, place two chairs a metre apart so they're facing each other. Loop the elastic around the front two legs of each chair to form a rectangular frame. With the elastic at ankle height, move the chairs wider apart until the elastic is taut. If you're playing with friends, ask them to face each other with the elastic stretched between them at ankle height.
Step 3. Get jumping! Everyone follows the same jumping sequence:
. Stand outside the elastics
. Jump so that your feet land on either side of the left elastic.
. Jump so your feet land on either side of the right elastic.
. Jump and land both feet inside the elastics.
. Jump and land both feet outside the elastics.
. Jump and land one foot on top of each elastic, pinning them down.
Once you've mastered the sequence, try double jumps, the 'bunny hop', full diamonds, and the twisty jump (see over the page). If you stumble or miss a step, it's the next person's turn.
Step 4. Try the next level. When you've done all the different styles at ankle height without a mistake, try it again with the elastics at mid-shin (and even knee!) height.

FROM THE ARCHIVES

Think about this: every time you jump, you're actually defying gravity! Gravity is the force that is always acting on you, keeping you on the ground instead of floating off into space, even when you're sitting or sleeping – but you'll only really feel it when you're jumping and come back down to land (that's gravity doing its thing). The physicist Isaac Newton explained this (and other phenomena that cause us to move or stop moving) in one of his Laws of Motion. His 'Law of Inertia' explains that an object in motion (in this case, you) will remain in motion unless it comes into contact with an outside force (in this case, gravity).

DEAR GROWN-UPS

Don't underestimate the game of elastics – have a try and you'll quickly come to appreciate the coordination, stamina and fitness required! It's a surprisingly multi-faceted game: there's gross and fine motor skills involved, foot/eye coordination needed, and rhymes to memorise – plenty of reasons to get jumping. Best of all, it's a game where fresh challenge keeps pace with developing mastery, so will pay dividends for as long as your elastic lasts.

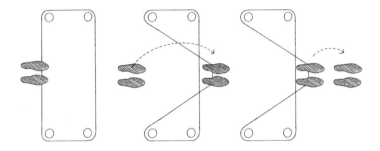

The bunny hop

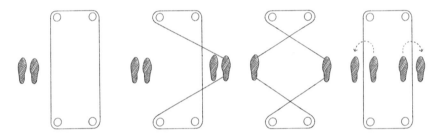

Full diamonds

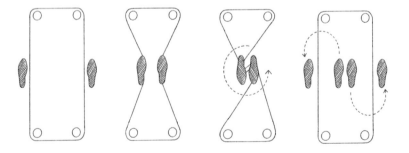

The twisty jump

Index

COOK SOMETHING

DO SOMETHING

ACKNOWLEDGEMENTS

Four children related to the team were born during the making of this book: Silas, Elis, Jad and Lily, and the team has a total of six children — thank you to them all for sharing their mummies.

I'm extremely grateful to my editor Clare for bringing out the best in me, for inspiring and supporting me, for all her wonderful contributions and for elevating the entire project.

To Sabrina for creating stunning illustrations that capture the Fanny & Alexander world perfectly, and for always having the capacity to surprise me while also staying true to our vision.

To Charlotte for her patience, understanding and for her clever solutions that so elevated our initial ideas about how this book might look.

To Hiromi for her adaptability, diligence, efficiency and dedication.

To Katja for intuitively understanding the project and making such delicious and nutritious seasonal recipes.

To John, Tristan, Anna Lisa and Anna for agreeing to contribute to our humble little book, for sharing their passions and for inspiring children with their infectious enthusiasm for their subjects.